LEADING PROJECTS

LEADING PROJECTS
A Manager's Pocket Guide

Trevor L Young

The Industrial Society

First published in 1993 by
The Industrial Society
Robert Hyde House
48 Bryanston Square
London W1H 7LN
Telephone: 071-262 2401

© *The Industrial Society 1993*

ISBN 0 85290 878 4

British Library Cataloguing-in-Publication Data.
A catalogue record for this book is available from the
British Library.

Typeset by: The Midlands Book Typesetting Company
Printed by: Cromwell Press
Cover design: Pylon

Text illustrations: Sophie Grillet

Contents

List of Figures

1

Project 'Change'?

Everyone lives and works in a rapidly changing environment and today most managers are aware of their responsibility to respond rapidly and effectively to changing business conditions. Attempting to control this process is now a priority activity for any innovative company.

In normal process management you attempt to control the day to day business operations which contribute to achieving the corporate objectives. Change is often a subtle, accumulative process which is accepted within the framework of normal operating activities. However, major changes in these activities can cause significant adverse reaction from people. It is impossible to ignore the changes that are happening inside and outside an organisation or their effects and consequences. If you can manage change in a pro-active way then you can minimise adverse reactions and consequences and contribute to making your organisation more successful.

To make this process effective you must respond rapidly to the signals indicating the need for change. How does your organisation react now? Is the accepted response, "We've always done it this way", or "It's worked O.K.·for the last five years." Do you and your colleague managers realise that to meet the new needs identified you cannot always respond within the framework of normal operations? This framework has tended to be restrictive, with the key elements of procedures, policies, reports, information systems and progress or performance measurement. To respond to the change you need to break down this framework and rebuild parts of it to meet the challenge of the future.

This process requires skills and techniques you are not likely to have used in normal operations. Traditions must be devalued, working practices questioned, people skills given greater emphasis and standards made flexible to the situation.

The skills you need in this situation have existed and been practised for several decades but generally confined to certain specialised business sectors. These are contained in the principles of Project Management. They are well tried and tested and comprise the sum of all the skills and techniques that can be used to control change at work effectively, in a formal structured way, to achieve desired results.

There is increasing pressure on all managers to use these skills and techniques and to identify a wide range of operating activities as 'special tasks' or Projects that contribute in a very positive way to the business achieving its strategic objectives. This creates a tendency for all work to become less 'operational' and more 'projectised' – broken down into packets of tasks to be completed with defined constraints. These projects may be short in duration, lasting a few days, or large and last over several months or even years. The number of people involved may vary from one to many hundreds and costs may similarly span a wide range.

Some examples of projects are:

- Writing a business or marketing plan
- Designing a new set of procedures
- Launching a new product
- Designing/installing new IT or computer systems
- Setting up a sales campaign
- Organising a sporting event
- Organising a fund raising event
- Organising an office layout or move
- A planned maintenance programme
- An annual training programme
- An audit or survey
- Restructuring an organisation
- Planning customised production
- Market research
- Developing new products and services

Each of these is a packet of tasks that together lead to an end result that is desired by the organisation in a specific time.

If the time taken to complete a project drifts uncontrolled the project does not achieve this result. Failure is perceived – often with unexpected consequences for the business and you!

The effects of failure could be far-reaching for the organisation. Suppose a planned office move takes place and staff then discover the computer services are still not fully operational. The current high dependency on computer support for most aspects of day to day operations means this failure could cost the company a significant loss of profit. Project Management is a process which uses many skills and techniques so that pre-planned events actually happen as intended at the outset. This process brings several of the characteristics of line management into sharper focus. These include:

- Objectives oriented
- Change oriented
- Frequently multi-disciplined
- Practical
- Opportunistic
- Questions tradition and values
- Performance oriented
- Control oriented

For many short or medium duration projects it is unlikely an organisation can justify setting up a separate project team with its own facilities and support services. Apart from cost the effects of removing people from their normal line duties is not acceptable.

You are expected to continue with your normal line management responsibilities while assuming the role of project manager for one or more projects.

In this role the you may have a project team comprising a mixed group of people drawn from different departments, divisions or even other organisations. This means your working arrangements have to be modified to meet the demands of day to day operations and also the project. Some of the people may be involved in more than one project at any given time, besides their responsibilities allocated by their functional line manager. Such teams are often transient, requiring a different mix of membership and skills at each stage as the project progresses.

So, Project Management is a convenient process to use in the control of change. It allows you to be effectively pro-active to meet the challenge of the changing needs of the organisation. A team effort is necessary and your effective management of the team and the process is essential from the start.

Effective leadership of the team is a prerequisite to achieving success with your project.

Summary

- *Managing change requires new skills*
- *Traditions must be devalued*
- *Flexibility to the situation is essential*
- *Project management is a process for managing change*
- *Project management is a pro-active process*

What is a Project?

A simple definition is just a 'special task'. This suggests it is something that is outside normal day to day operating activities. In practice operational work is made up of day to day activities which are familiar to those who do the work. They are using existing skills and experience. These capabilities are combined together in a group of people in such a way that they work well together to produce the desired results. This is teamwork with the effort directed towards the results needed by the organisation at the time.

The team leader has a 'doing' role, co-ordinating the efforts of the team and doing some of the work. Generally the work of the team is pre-determined by the needs of the organisation through the functional line structure that is familiar to everybody. Established rules and work practices exist and administration procedures are designed to cope with the known range of problems and activities based on experience.

Smooth operation is the aim of all managers at all levels, seeking to be pro-active where possible. When unexpected situations arise that demand immediate reaction, experience has established ways of dealing with the problem in order to get a speedy return to smooth working again – until the next crisis hits! When the problem cannot be resolved with established methods and practices the organisation is faced with a change. A new approach is needed to enable everybody to attempt to maintain a state of equilibrium – smooth working prevails again.

It is when the organisation realises the new approach is needed the magic words 'special task' pop up. The new approach is separated from the day to day activities if only for the reason that the team are too busy to devote time to coming up with a solution. It is apparent that the problem has appeared before in other departments but time constraints have given the need to attempt a solution a low priority. Perhaps the skills and experience that are perceived to exist now in the organisation are inadequate to resolve the problem. New methods, tools and techniques are possibly required and additional skills and capabilities are needed in their application. The 'special task' starts to take on a new appearance. It is suddenly something unique and special and it is realised that there is a definite need to carry out this task in a different manner from normal day to day operations.

Some new dimensions appear that have values special to this task. Time and cost are given a high profile and attempts are made to define the desired outcome from the work. Presumably the results will be used and incorporated into the normal smooth working operations. So everything that happens during the execution of the 'special task' is regarded as part of a temporary group of activities, unique to the task and set apart from operations. The 'special task' has been born as a PROJECT.

The project therefore has defined constraints and specified results required by the organisation.

A project can be defined as;

... A GROUP OF ACTIVITIES WHICH ARE CARRIED OUT WITHIN A CLEARLY DEFINED TIME AND COST TO REACH A SET OF SPECIFIC OBJECTIVES.

A project has particular characteristics:

- Has a specific purpose
- It is usually not routine
- Comprises interdependent activities
- Has defined time constraints
- Often complex
- Has defined cost constraints
- Subject to cancellation
- Flexible to respond to further change
- Involves many unknowns
- Involves risk

Projects are traditionally perceived as highly technical activities carried out by engineers and technologists to build a recognisable result such as roads, bridges, hotels, office complexes, rockets, satellites etc. Such projects are technical and have all the characteristics identified above.

In most organisations managers have projects that are smaller in size and duration. They are not necessarily very technical in engineering or scientific content, but retain most of the characteristics of a project.

The project is a special anomaly in day to day operations. It often has to evolve, change shape or direction and respond to the organisational needs as they change. But the project depends on mutual effort by everybody involved in a controlled way if the desired results are to be achieved. The tools, techniques and methods employed to manage all projects are the same and only differ in their selection and application depending on the duration and complexity of the work. Complex analytical planning and monitoring tools are not usually selected for use on short projects that involve only a few people. Other simpler methods and procedures are applicable with such projects, whereas control of the project expected to last many months would benefit from using such rigorous tools.

Types of Projects

Projects can be divided into two broad categories:

- **HARD**
- **SOFT**

There is no clear definition of each type because many 'soft' projects eventually become 'hard' in the latter stages of the project. A project may start with only general objectives in line with the corporate needs. Then the project will seek to explore many options to get a solution to a particular problem. Once an agreed option is identified the project team will concentrate on that particular option and work to achieve the desired result. The project starts at the conceptual stage with vague boundaries and limits. This allows flexibility and a creative climate to prevail. As the work of the project progresses the soft edges of the project boundaries start to take a more defined shape. The objectives become clearer and specific, and realistic deadlines for achieving results are agreed. The initial softness of the project disappears and a 'hard' project develops. These projects frequently occur in most organisations.

Examples are;

- Developing a new product
- Developing new packaging for existing products
- Designing new procedures and systems
- Designing new product brochures

These projects are 'soft' at the start, with a high level of uncertainty of achieving the desired result. Often the result is not clearly known or defined. There are many unknowns explored to derive a range of alternatives, each of which are then examined in more detail. This process involves the leader and the team in non-routine activities, many of them taking a significant amount of time due to lack of familiarity. It often requires the application of new, specialised skills that are rapidly acquired to carry out the work. The skills needed for the project are not easily identified at the start. At some stage new skills may be needed that are acquired from outside the team or even the organisation.

Fig. 2.1 gives some common properties for each category of project.

HARD PROJECTS	SOFT PROJECTS
Clearly defined objectives	Objectives broadly stated
Scope identified	Scope wide open intentionally
Constraints generally known	Many constraints unknown at start
Specifications established at start	Specifications part of project
Planning based on past experience	Planning limited at start - little experience
Skills required known at start	Skills required assessed continually
Resources readily identified	Resources not easily identified at start
Base plan fixed at start	Base plan difficult to establish
Control Process usually in place	Control Process custom designed
Quality standards exist	Quality standards written during project
Performance standards fixed at start	Performance standards flexible
Team structuring during planning	Team structuring flexible
Organisation for projects established	Organisation for projects missing
Risk limited and predictable	Risk unpredictable
Success criteria agreed at start	Success criteria change with time
Project cost defined at start	Project cost difficult to define
Project duration fixed at start	Project duration flexible
Constant leadership	Leaderhip moves during project

Fig. 2.1   Properties of Projects

Summary

- *A project is a special task outside day to day operating activities*
- *It involves activities which have clearly defined limits of time and cost*
- *It has clearly defined objectives*
- *Projects can be divided into two types – hard and soft*

3

The Role of the Project Leader

As a project comprises a unique set of activities combined to achieve specific objectives, your role as the project leader is often complex. It probably only occupies part of your daily routine as a manager. It is outside the traditionally accepted line hierarchy in the organisation and requires links to your colleagues and managers at all levels. These links are specifically only for the work of the project during its life and create a large number of short term relationships which form part of a matrix.

This matrix embraces the small team assigned to the project. They are dedicated to spend a large part of their time on the project. This is in contrast to many other people at all levels in various functional areas who have inputs to make, who are not operating with similar priorities to the project team. The co-ordination of the efforts of all these people and the project team is an essential part of your role as the project leader.

For the project to progress you have to respond to changing needs and demands in ways which are not always clearly defined within established procedures or accepted practices. These usually do not exist either formally or informally. In practice you will probably need to adopt methods, in the interests of the project, which break across accepted boundaries and confront the traditions and culture of the organisation. At times you will feel left outside the normal hierarchy in the role, vulnerable to opposition from people at all levels whom you previously regarded as your colleagues and friends. You may even be perceived as interfering with the normal, smooth operation of the business.

Operating Characteristics

As the project leader you are:
- Responsible for achieving project objectives
- Clearly in charge and in a position of high risk
- Limited in authority to get resources internally & externally
- Expected to get results, cutting across established customs
- Operating in unknown and unpredictable areas
- Susceptible to low credibility with other managers
- Regarded with distrust by those not involved

As the leader you are obliged to operate in an environment where you must:
- Examine self performance continually
- Ensure team leadership stays positive

- Manage the client, end users and all those with an interest
- Manage project integration and interfaces
- Ensure the expectations of all those involved are satisfied
- Monitor progress and track project targets and deadlines
- Ensure plans are accurate
- Keep resource levels in line with plans
- Maintain senior management commitment
- Attend to teamworking to maintain high performance

So you have a difficult role to fulfil with many operating areas and activities that rarely, if ever, are of major concern in hierarchical line management. A priority for you is to 'manage' all those people who have an interest in the project at any stage of the project life cycle, regardless of their level of involvement. If success is to be achieved then the effective management of performance is essential at all stages of the project life.

There are three functional areas to your new role:

- Managing all those with an interest in the project
- Managing each phase of the project effectively
- Managing performance of the people

The whole group of people and institutions who share some stake or an interest in the project is known as the project stakeholders. The extent of interest and influence by the stakeholders can have a marked effect on the final outcome of the project. Generally project success is very dependent on effective management of these people. Neglecting them will invariably hinder the achievement of project objectives as your ability to manage performance effectively will be restricted.

Summary

- *Your role as project leader is additional to your normal operating duties*
- *You frequently have to operate in a matrix for your project*
- *You must manage the project stakeholders*
- *You must effectively manage the project through its separate phases*
- *You are responsible for performance throughout the whole process*

4

The Project Window

If you are fortunate enough to have an office with a window to the outside, take a look now from where you are sitting. What do you see? If you don't have a window try your boss's office! The view you see now depends on your position relative to the window. Initial perception is based on the central area observed and the nature of the surroundings.

If your present position is some distance from the window the amount of information available to you is limited. It is constrained by the window frame. Other data closer to you are within reach to interfere with the information available through the window. If this additional, nearby data are interesting to you they will cause distraction from the window view. You are likely to feel more comfortable with the nearby data because they are familiar, such as furniture and people who are known to you – maybe even members of your own team.

If you now move closer to the window the whole situation changes. The view through the window expands and much more information becomes available to you. It is likely that the whole view cannot be taken in at one glance. You must scan from left to right, up and down in order to get all the information available from this new position. Repeated scans may be necessary to gather all the information because your situation has changed. At the same time the view is more interesting as it is enlarged and the nearby data are of less interest. This interest and curiosity leads you even closer to the window to ensure the whole view is available. As this happens you become absorbed with the information available in the window. There is a tendency to shut out the other data which previously interfered with the visual messages received by you. You have become involved with all the information presented through the window, shutting out local distractions.

The same circumstances apply to leading a project. When you are appointed as the leader the project window makes it's first appearance. At this point the window is probably quite small because it is distant. The project data available are limited, often just a general description or 'Terms of Reference' which may be supported by a feasibility study carried out much earlier. The project specification is probably vague – "to allow flexibility". Little planning has been carried out and no-one has any real idea what is involved.

The project will certainly have some objectives, although these are not always immediately obvious to you. The stated objectives are often unclear and sometimes even misguided. Availability of resources has probably received

little attention but there could be a budget limit set. So the view through the window is very limited. The information available to you is constrained by personal and organisational influences of those involved at the conceptual stage of the project. You will have many distractions at this point, principally day to day operational activities. These have to continue and the project role is an additional burden for you which can lead to additional stress.

If the project is to get a good start, you have to move quickly closer to the window. The view is confusing and hazy because there are many unknowns so only a few steps forward can be taken. At an early stage you will consider the resources available and start to assemble the core team for the project. This may comprise people from your own team or close associates. At this stage the window appears as shown in Fig. 4.1.

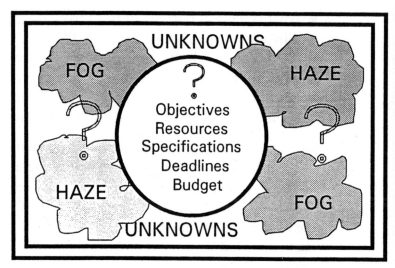

Fig. 4.1   The Project Window – first view

The next major leap forward is the key to the success of the whole project. It is made up of two giant steps:

- Getting the project in context
- Identifying all those with an interest in the project

The window currently gives little or no information on either and you cannot start the planning process without these inputs to enlarge the view.

Getting the project in context

Both you and the core team need to be clear on the context of the project in the overall organisation. You need answers to questions such as:

- How does this fit into corporate strategy?
- Why is it necessary?
- What has been done before?

- What is the real purpose of this project?
- Why are we selected for the project?
- What will we gain from the project if it succeeds?
- What happens if we fail?
- What will the organisation gain from the project?
- What are the expectations of the senior management?

Getting answers to these and many other similar fact finding questions creates a vision for the project and removes some of the haze in the project window. The core team will become 'involved' with the project, gaining acceptance of the need for their future efforts. They will understand the reasons behind the project and the risks to be faced in the process of change that the project is to achieve. This is the first great step you take to build commitment in the project team.

Identifying the Stakeholders

The stakeholders comprise a group of people who have an interest in the project. This starts with you and the core team since your interest is obvious. In every project the interest in the results is not limited to this group. There are always many others with a vested interest in all or parts of the project life-cycle as well as the results achieved finally.

Every project will have a sponsor, a senior manager who is directly sponsoring the project and is often accountable at senior level (see Section 7). With the help of your team you must then assess all the possible stakeholders who have an interest from the start or who will have an interest at a later stage.

Some of these are shown in Fig. 4.2. Always ask: "Who

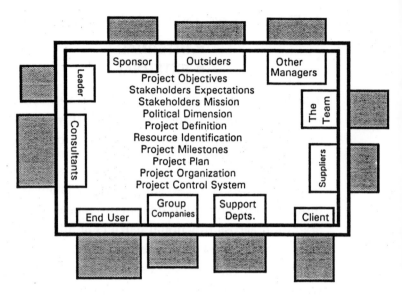

Fig. 4.2   The Project Window with Stakeholders

could possibly have any interest in this project, now or later?".

Each project has its own group of stakeholders and it is clearly important to try to identify them all at this early stage. All of them have an input to make and they will all have a different perception of the needs, purpose and objectives of the project. All will have different expectations for widely differing reasons.

The stakeholders have their own individual strategy, mission and strengths and weaknesses. Each has their own hidden agenda, in the same way as you and your team members, who as individuals, have aspirations to personal gain from their involvement. These are the grey areas shown in Fig. 4.2 representing the unknown data presently outside the project window.

As Fig. 4.2 shows, the stakeholders fall into two groups:

- **INTERNAL**
- **EXTERNAL**

You have first to secure the support and commitment of the internal stakeholders. Since they all work for the same organisation this is theoretically preset by the decision to proceed with the project.

In practice this is not so simple. There is always a political dimension to be considered that influences the degree of co-operation across functional barriers at all levels. You often have to work hard to secure the support and commitment the project needs for success. The project has to compete with other projects as well as day to day operations to acquire the essential resources. Other colleague managers may believe they should have the project responsibility because they believe they could do a better job. There is a high competitive element in such situations which can create difficult relationships and conflict for you.

The external stakeholders cover a wide range of possibilities from the end user and client (who may not be the same), to the local community, external institutions, suppliers, consultants and contractors. Their influence may be central or on the fringes, at the start or much later in the project life cycle.

You have limited authority over many of these stakeholders and will often have difficulty influencing them to advantage. It is a formidable challenge to manage them effectively and ensure they remain positive in supporting you to achieve the project objectives.

Summary

- *Derive the project window for your project*
- *Understand the project in corporate context – ask questions*
- *Identify all the project stakeholders – list them as Internal and External*
- *Ensure you obtain senior management support and commitment at this early stage*

5

The Effective Project Leader

As the project leader you are working to get results with and through other people – the project team. One key element to success is your ability to energise and direct this diverse group to give high performance, willingly, throughout the project life.

The individuals in the team come from different parts of the organisation and have different priorities, experiences, skills and interests. In many organisations different departments have their own departmental culture, created by the manager. Inter-departmental barriers exist as departments protect their interests. You have to overcome these barriers and create a climate of co-operation and co-ordinate the team's efforts successfully. You must *lead* and also *motivate* the members of the project team often with minimal legitimate line authority over their actions.

To be seen as an effective project leader you have to orchestrate the work, manage the numerous inter-departmental interfaces, seek and co-ordinate all the skills necessary to achieve results. You have to manage *the process* aspects of project management as well as the people involved. The process is dependent on identifying the right skills necessary for the project at any particular time and ensuring they are used effectively in accordance with the plans and schedules.

To do this you must have these process skills and a clear understanding of the tools and techniques used to make the process run smoothly. This suggests you are superhuman with all the skills to do the job alone! This is clearly not possible in practice, although some do try with regrettable results. The answer is in your ability to hold on to control of the project process, to know what is happening when and where and be ready to take appropriate action when problems appear.

Project management is a vogue expression in today's business world. The pressure on most types of business to produce results on time within strict time constraints has led to the need for a breed of managers with specific skills. The wide range of these skills and competences justifies project management being regarded as a profession. It is considered that a manager with good people skills and a broad understanding of the purpose of the project is naturally capable of leading a project successfully. But is this simple assumption really true?

Many managers are expected to take responsibility for projects with little or no additional specialist training or understanding of the skills required. This is a short sighted approach that can lead to disaster. Project management should be regarded as a core competency for management development of professional managers today. If you feel that your level of skills for the job is not adequate to give you a strong sense of self confidence then seek additional training now.

Leadership theories

Numerous theories and models of leadership have been proposed. Leadership has always been associated with the individual having a range of relevant qualities or traits, intentionally developed or inherited, that make that individual stand apart from others. But in practice the qualities, characteristics and skills required in a leader are really determined by the demands of the situation in which they are required to perform. There is much evidence in recent history that qualities alone are insufficient to qualify someone for a position of leadership. The characteristics you have must bear some close relationship to the work to be performed, the results desired and the characteristics, activities and objectives of those who must follow. This is not a denial of qualities because you must have above average knowledge in many relevant aspects of the work done by the team, combined with self-assurance, status and a strong sense of responsibility.

Everyone is an individual in the way the job is done. Everyone has a particular behaviour pattern which is influenced by many factors, both intrinsic and extrinsic. Although most people display a range of behaviour patterns it is common to examine such behaviour at two extremes of a spectrum. How does an individual behave when everything is going really well? How does that same individual behave when things are going badly? The examination of these situations and the various intermediate states gives valuable information about an individual's *style of leadership*. A leader adopts a particular style according to the prevailing situation or in anticipation of a situation that is expected to develop.

Many of the theories of leadership style are derived with methods of analysis based on questionnaires. The results are varied, but in most there are elements of truth which can help you learn something about how you would tend to behave in different situations. Style theories are usually based on the range of behaviours perceived between total autocracy and democracy. The style adopted in any situation has an important impact on the members of the project team. The extremes of style can be summarised as:

■ Autocratic leader

You *dictate* what should be done, how and when. Beyond that you expect things to be done and avoid being involved in problem solving or external influences on the progress of the work. You are only really interested to know that the tasks are complete on time.

■ Democratic leader

If autocratic leadership is the traditional style then the democratic style is the contemporary approach to maximum participation. You *involve* everybody in all aspects of the team's activities. There is more discussion and consultation in decision making and taking. Team member skills and creativity are actively encouraged by you creating a climate to help everybody achieve project, team and personal goals.

■ **Laissez-faire leader**

It is worth mentioning this style which is often found to exist in practice. This leadership style describes you when you have effectively *abdicated* into the team. All the team members work on their own as independent units, including you. The team is no longer a team but becomes a *work group* with only personal objectives dominant. Team spirit and project objectives are lost in a fog of indecision, poor planning and inadequate co-ordination of effort. Project success is unlikely with the group members behaving in sometimes unpredictable ways to protect themselves.

It is widely recognised that a participative style is preferred in most organisations because it allows the employees to feel involved in their work. This is a major element of motivation at work. In project work a participative style is certain to yield better results, if only because of the wide range of skills employed at each stage of the project process. Participative leaders are not afraid to get their hands soiled by doing some of the work with the team. When the need arises you adopt a high enough profile and position to make your power and influence felt to the benefit of the project and the team.

The key challenge for you as the project leader today is to anticipate changing situations and respond appropriately, using available skills in the team to keep the project momentum towards its objectives. You can only respond to

this challenge with actions in all parts of the project process to get results. This *functional approach* is essential to project leadership. The action-centred leadership developed by John Adair (*Effective Leadership*, Gower Press, 1983) identifies the functions of an effective leader with a balance between the needs of the team, the individuals and the tasks they are performing. These are related in a simple model shown in Fig. 5.1 that shows how all the actions you take as a leader fall into three inter-linked functional areas. The core area of overlap of all three areas or circles in the diagram indicates the overview that you must take to maintain control. In project management the process of control pervades all aspects of the work in the team and the stakeholders.

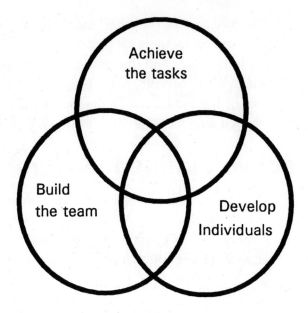

Fig. 5.1   Action-centred leadership

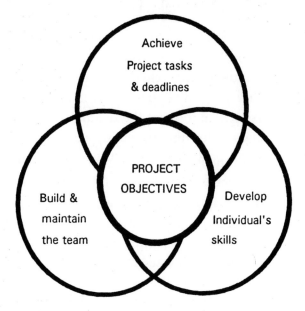

Fig. 5.2   Objectives directed leadership

The core area of the Adair model must therefore include a more specific activity for projects. All the efforts of the team, the individuals and the tasks they carry out are directed to one specific outcome, the project objectives. So the core area of the model can be overlaid with an additional circle labelled *Project Objectives* as illustrated in Fig. 5.2.

Objective directed leadership

The project leader is in a position to ensure that the project objectives are kept in high profile at all times and keep the project process going in the right direction. In this process you are constantly monitoring that:

- Scheduled work is carried out
- Deadlines are met on time
- The team is working well together
- All individuals are equipped with the skills needed

You are always moving between the three functional areas co-ordinating the work, making sure the team has sufficient resources and is clear about its purpose and responsibilities. Any individual having problems will need guidance or assistance to meet the deadlines and complete the current tasks. Throughout these activities you are concerned to stand back and take an overview from the centre, to see that everything is going to plan.

If you are confined to these areas of activity then the project process is likely to be effectively under control. But you are operating in a confined situation – the inner workings of the project process – and are therefore *inner directed*.

Earlier it was concluded that you also have to manage all those with an interest in the project throughout its life. These stakeholders are on the outer fringes of the project process as most are probably not involved in the day to day operating activities of the project team. Yet they can influence the project directly and indirectly and must be brought into your sphere of operating control.

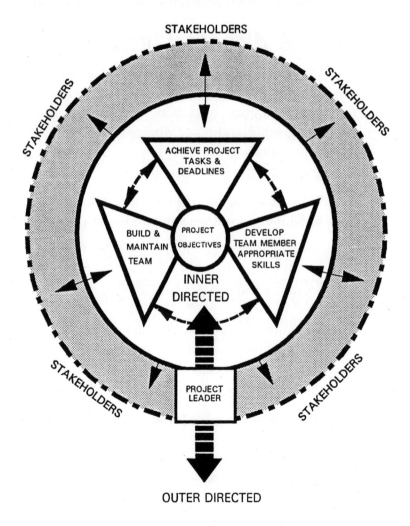

Fig. 5.3 The Objective-centred Project Leader

The stakeholders must be 'managed' by you if overall project control is to be effectively maintained at all times. So apart from concern for the inner working of the project process, you must expand your sphere of influence. All the stakeholders must be brought into the operating area and your efforts must also become *outer directed*.

As the project leader you are therefore faced with the holistic role of managing and controlling the project process, the team, the team members and all the stakeholders to achieve the objectives. This is achieved in practice by your continual migration between the two positions of being inner and outer directed, balancing the needs and expectations of each area to reach the objectives. This is shown on the leadership model in Fig. 5.3.

This wide ranging role brings additional pressures on you to have good influencing and negotiating skills to keep all the elements in balance. The potential for conflicts arising is fairly high as the individual agendas of everybody involved surface over particular issues, problems and projected plans. You need tact and diplomacy but good communication skills are clearly essential for this balancing process to succeed.

The Leader's action cycle

At every stage of the project you will follow a process which has five basic steps. This process is applicable to the project as a whole through the four basic phases of the project life. It is equally applicable to any individual part of the project plan such as one key task to be completed.

STEP 1

Defining the objectives and deadlines – You need to define the overall project and task objectives, at the same time making sure that the team understands these in context. You must take particular care at this point to ensure that everyone can accept their involvement in the work ahead as this is essential to building commitment. Deadlines form an integral part of these short, medium or long term objectives with clearly identified results and the benefits expected. The scope of the project is specified and you demonstrate your own commitment and enthusiasm for the project.

STEP 2

Preparing the plan and schedules – With clear objectives established the planning process usually follows two stages – fact finding and decision taking. In each you will involve the team members as a team building activity. This helps you to create the right climate for generating acceptance and commitment to the work to be carried out.

- **Fact finding** is an information gathering process to ensure that all relevant data are collected together for the planning process. You encourage ideas and suggestions to be tabled and consult with team members, colleagues and others to generate all available relevant data on any particular aspect of the project. This will comprise a mixture of historical experience, facts, opinions and legend which has to be sorted and filtered to provide really useful data.

- **Decision taking** is the process of drawing conclusions for action from the alternatives and options generated in the consultative stage. This signals the termination of gathering data and using the data to generate the plans in a format which everyone can use and understand. The presentation of this information will vary in complexity according to who needs it and how it is to be used. In certain types of projects it is often prudent to keep some options available as contingencies if a recognised possible sequence of events does occur.

STEP 3

Briefing the team and stakeholders – Having identified all the activities of the plan it is essential you inform everybody involved what has to be done, when things are to be done and the deadlines. This stage is vital to generating 'ownership' in the team and the stakeholders. You need to know that each individual clearly understands their responsibilities and what is expected of them in the implementation stage. Of course it is not practical to give all the detail at the start-up. In fact some of this will not even be available as many of the work plans will only be developed as the project proceeds. Each team member must clearly understand their role and the points of interface with other team members and stakeholders that they have to manage during the project.

STEP 4

Monitoring progress and support – You have established the climate and environment for the work to proceed. You must now ensure motivation is maintained at a high level, dealing promptly with problems as they arise. These may be technical, administrative or resource problems and you will need to take the migratory position between being 'inner' and 'outer' directed to keep everything in balance. This involves you in 'management by walking about' to keep yourself well informed on what is happening and giving support, guidance and assistance where necessary. This visible leadership is essential to encourage the team and show an interest in their welfare and progress. You will not be in a position of control by adopting a distant position – 'management by walking away'. This will lead to poor teamwork and you being poorly informed of the real state of affairs with the project progress.

STEP 5

Evaluating results – Evaluation is not a terminal activity! Although you will surely evaluate the performance at the end of the project you must actively evaluate on a day to day basis. Through regular contact with the team and the stakeholders you determine if the project is on the right track and the results are meeting expectations. You can identify if the planning process you have carried out was effective, correct and comprehensive to meet these needs. Through this active evaluation you can determine if changes are necessary and take steps to implement modifications to your plans. When the project finally reaches the declared point of completion then you carry out a full post-project evaluation to appraise the performance of yourself and the team throughout the project. It is important to identify the key learning points gained from experience during the project and record these for future reference.

These five steps can be regarded as a cyclic process within the four phases of a project from conception through to termination. They apply to the project in total and any dependent group of tasks. This is shown in Fig. 5.4.

In practice the action cycle is a multitude of cycles, each

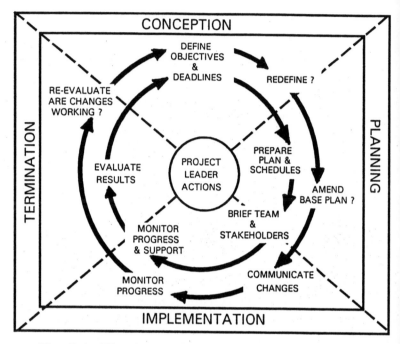

Fig. 5.4   The Action Cycle in the project life cycle

at different stages of progress. At any time blockages can appear to interfere and cause a hold up. This may be due to new information becoming available, poor fact finding initially or just poor communications within the team and between the team and the stakeholders. You may find the objectives revised as one or more stakeholders 'move the goal posts' without informing you in good time to prevent wasted effort. Your plans may show shortcomings as the team comes up with better ideas and you must decide whether to modify the schedules.

In fact at any stage of any cycle there is the possibility that the processes may need repeating to resolve problems and derive ways to bypass the blockages. This is a dynamic process that enables you to maintain control and keep the project momentum. These five steps are the key results areas where you take action as project leader to achieve ultimate success.

Summary

The effective project leader is:
- *Inner directed to achieve the objectives*
- *Outer directed to manage the stakeholders*
- *Concerned to achieve the project tasks on time*
- *Concerned to build a well co-ordinated team*
- *Concerned to seek appropriate skills in the team for the project*
- *Operating in a dynamic environment of taking actions through the four phases of the project*

6

The Project Life Cycle

The concept of 'life cycles' is well known, particularly in product marketing where a product history can be traced from conception to end of viable life in producing profits for an organisation. This concept is applicable to projects and in a similar way all projects follow a systems approach through the four basic phases of any project to the end point. The leader's action cycle is readily contained within the larger framework of the project life with these identifiable phases.

These can conveniently be illustrated in a chart form with the two dimensions of time versus some other factor such as effort, cost, resources, or conflict. The project phases take on an important characteristic – the life cycle. When the four phases are complete the project is finished and the participating members may move back to the start of the cycle and prepare for the next project. In practice the cycle may repeat itself with a different leader and a different team, but in organisational terms the cycle repeats itself on a continuous basis with many projects in different phases at any point in time. This is one of the principal reasons why it is important for the organisation to establish a recognisable structure for projects (see Section 7).

Each of these four phases is distinct and the project process follows an identifiable flow through each. As project leader you must follow this flow path through each phase to reach a successful conclusion.

Phase 1 – Conception

The primary phase of all projects. At this initial stage the problem or need is identified and a decision made if there is a requirement for a project. The source may be the research department, from perceived problems in the current organisation, work practices or the organisational interfaces. There are many potential sources of identifying a potential project including staff committees, a manager's whims, Quality Teams, departmental team meetings, existing clients, Sales department through new or potential clients and in some instances even suggestion schemes.

This is really a critical stage since it is important that an organisation or procedure is established to process the need for some action to be taken. It is the fundamental step where a decision must be made that there is a need to do something.

Questions must be asked to make a judgement on whether

there is any real requirement to establish a project. The problem or need may be readily resolved within a department as part of its normal day to day operations with conventional problem solving techniques. If it is considered that the skills necessary exist in that department and a result can be achieved quickly without involving other functional areas there may be no necessity to establish 'project status'.

Conversely a clearly perceived need to involve other departments, external people and organisations and a wide spectrum of skills is more likely to dictate the need to establish a project. It is at this stage that a feasibility study may be requested by senior management as part of a justification procedure for the project to proceed. Any project activity is costly in terms of people's time and the possible interference or disruption of participants' normal work, so it important that at this point a further check is made. Any suggestion for a potential project must be clearly identified in context:

- Does it fit with the organisation's overall strategy?
- Can the decision to carry out a feasibility study itself be justified?
- Who is going to do the work, how and when?

The Feasibility Study

The first step is obviously your appointment to carry out the feasibility study. This does not necessarily mean you will be the project leader if the project does proceed eventually, although this is a probable outcome. It is important that you establish your terms of reference, particularly your authority in the investigative work you must carry out.

Your first step is to derive a 'Problem statement' based on the information from the source of the idea, need or problem identification. This is the primary element of your ultimate objective statement and leads you through the process of fact finding to establish the history, precedents and opinions (including prejudices) about the topic or problem. This is equivalent to 'picture painting' where the whole scene is gradually exposed piece by piece through your investigations.

The main factors to be included in the feasibility analysis are:

■ **Fact finding** – Questioning people to establish the background to the problem or need. This forms the basis of any subsequent idea generation activities you may employ to generate alternatives.

■ **Alternative methods** – Generating different possible ways to approach the resolution of the problem or need. This is essential for the filtration process you will employ to reduce these options to just two or three. It is common to derive three options – the apparent best, the most readily acceptable and the least worst in terms of effect on the organisation and people. You will set out a summary of how you arrived at these options, giving reasons and arguments to support your preferences.

■ **Economic evaluation** – You identify the costs likely to be incurred in the process of resolving the problem or need. These are costs of people, time, materials, equipment, revenue, overhead and capital costs. You may also need to identify similar costs for implementing the solution. As part of the justification process you work out the cost effect of the benefits which at this stage you reasonably expect the project to provide. This may be just savings but could be increased income generated. This is necessary to assist establishing success criteria and the measurement of performance.

■ **Source of finance** – You may need to consider funding arrangements or the amendments to budgets necessary to accommodate the expected project costs. You establish what level of approval is required and how long this will take to achieve. You also assess whether there is any income or saving generated as the project proceeds. A budget for the potential project is established with contingencies openly included. You may also have to derive a potential cash flow statement.

■ **Effects on current operations** – You analyse the effect of withdrawing effort for day to day operations from those functional areas you expect to give input and support to the potential project. There may be a significant cost penalty on those departments because of the reduced resources available for specific periods of time. If the result is locating external help, part time or temporary staff, this could impose an additional cost on the project itself. You will determine the range and type of skills you expect to use on the project and then determine their availability within the organisation. If these skills are not readily available then you must appraise the cost of importing them as required. The conclusions you derive must include action plans to minimise the adverse effects of the implementation of the project on normal day to day business operations.

■ **Assumptions made** – It is inevitable that you will have to make some assumptions during the work of feasibility analysis. It is important to define these assumptions clearly so that there is no doubt with anyone involved about your approach and the underlying reasons for your decisions. These assumptions may relate to such topics as the priorities set, the risks involved, organisational structure changes and levels of authority.

This initial evaluation will conclude with a summary of forecasts of potential gains and threats, estimates of cost and time and the context with basic organisational strategy. An initial statement of objectives is derived based on the available information. The use of problem solving techniques establishes whether or not the problem or need is clearly identified and whether or not it is a false perception that hides the real need. The project objectives are then defined and expectations of the outcomes established with outline plans describing how these are to be achieved.

This whole process is a paper study producing the feasibility report. This forms the basis of a corporate decision to proceed although there may be a considerable time lapse before this actually happens. If this occurs then some of the report contents may become suspect and even invalid due to environmental changes. Before initiating any project the information collected to make the decisions that are taken to proceed does need verification. This is your first action upon appointment as the project leader in the process of establishing clear objectives.

Phase 2 – Planning

With objectives identified you next proceed to the planning phase which comprises two stages, information gathering and taking decisions. Planning is about creating something that does not presently exist. You must therefore start to assemble a team of people.

You select and negotiate for the services of the people you believe have the skills, experience and ability to do the work you anticipate having to carry out in the future. These people form the 'core team' who will probably stay on the project through most or all of its life. You decide the direction you will go with your team to reach the objectives. With this team you seek answers to various questions, principally:

- What do we need to do?
- How are we going to do it?
- When do we need to do each part?
- Where are we going to do it?
- What are we **not** going to do?

Out of the fact finding process you derive detailed plans and schedules to carry out the work that will lead to the desired outcomes defined in the objectives statement. Budgets are established for all the stages of the plan and resource needs analysed in detail. Individual responsibilities are decided and the corresponding work plans set out. As part of this phase of the project you establish administrative procedures that you and the team are to employ, particularly reporting, feedback and control systems.

Phase 3 – Execution

At the start of implementing the project you will have to be sure that your plans are detailed enough to allow an immediate and confident start. You ensure that all the team members clearly understand their responsibilities and the work practices and procedures that are jointly agreed. This project organisation is essential to an effective start.

The actual work planned is carried out and at all stages the progress is monitored and measured against the original plan. Variances are identified and corrective action taken where appropriate to keep the project on the right track. Where necessary you involve the relevant stakeholders, particularly where significant changes are clearly needed. Performance is verified at each stage. Regular progress reporting is essential at all levels to maintain the commitment and support of everybody.

Phase 4 – Termination

As the project approaches a recognisable completion point you can start the handover to the end user or client. This

is often a staged process involving various approvals and possibly staff training. Project evaluation is carried out and a final report issued. The project run-down may identify various ongoing support and maintenance activities that you must take action to establish before the completion point. Before the team is dispersed to other activities you have your final opportunity to carry out the last evaluation exercise. There are valuable lessons and learning points to gather together and record for future projects. This data can be lost and forgotten unless you act at this point.

Management

Each phase involves a wide range of activities within an organisation requiring inputs from various functions and different levels. Each of the phases frequently needs to pass through several stages before completion. In these conditions 'life cycle management' is an essential process. It particularly emphasises the different management requirements at each phase of a dynamic process. Traditional organisation structures are not necessarily suited to effective management of a project. The structure must be designed to cope with the changing environment that the project meets at each stage and each phase of the work.

The matrix structure that is often denounced by organisations for operating a business is a reality for a major part of the project life. Your role in effectively managing the project process in this type of structure is one of the critical factors for success.

Each phase of the life cycle has associated specific actions that need to be carried out. This can only be done if the organisation structure is appropriate and senior management

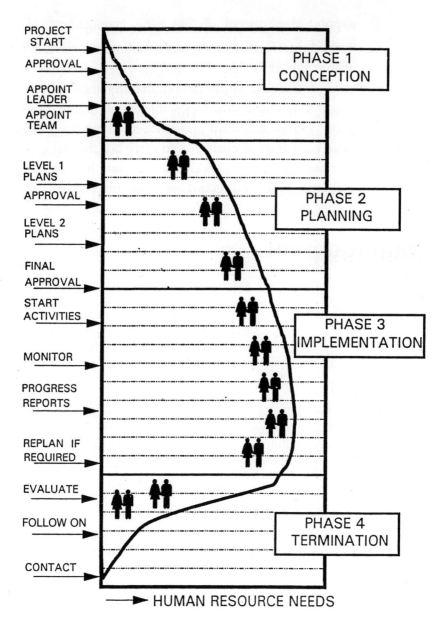

Fig. 6.1   The Project life cycle

support the concept of 'life cycle management'. Fig. 6.1 illustrates the project life cycle to show how different dimensions can be plotted against time.

The amount of effort associated with each phase varies through the life cycle. This organisational effort can be measured as hours, money or assets deployed. With one of these or other factors as the 'y' axis the concept does provide the organisation with a useful data bank on the variation and usage of such factors at each phase for different projects.

Summary

Every project has a life cycle of our phases

- *Projects are CONCEIVED to satisfy a need*
- *Ensure you understand how the project fits in with corporate strategy*
- *Check all aspects of feasibility reports before deriving the project objectives*
- *PLANNING involves factfinding, making decisions and paying attention to detail*
- *EXECUTION of the project requires detailed plans, schedules, organisation and procedures*
- *TERMINATION is the structured run-down to handover, evaluation and identified follow on*

7

The Project Structure

A project involves a collection of people, materials, equipment, data and information or other attributes. These are grouped together in a particular way by a carefully designed framework to achieve the objectives. Thus the project is a system, which can be broken down into sub-systems or principal parts, each of which can be broken down further into sub-sets of component parts or tasks. If any part is missing the project is no longer whole and cannot achieve the objectives. The project that is carefully organised and managed is greater than just the sum of the parts, because of the impact of the results as they develop on other parts of the organisation.

Project management is a dynamic process and the project system is a sub-system of the organisational system. Inside the project there is a need for a high level of close interfacing between the sub-systems and component parts or tasks. The organisation itself is the sum total of all its sub-systems, one of which is your project which has its own sub-set of interfaces inside and outside the organisation.

It is fundamental to the success of the project that a structure exists that clearly shows the organisational system and the interfaces with the project which must be managed. These interfaces have boundary limits which need definition to avoid confusion and allow good project control. Within the organisation the interfaces usually involve from one to three different levels starting at or near the top of the management structure where the strategic decision taking process is centred.

Typically the three levels are:

- **A Sponsor**
- **An Accountable Executive**
- **A Project Leader**

The scope and strategic importance of the project determine which level of management fulfils these three roles in practice. Their relative positions in the hierarchy does not necessarily affect their responsibilities in managing the organisational interfaces.

If there are many projects within the organisational system, each at different phases of the life cycle, then it may be appropriate to have a Project Steering Committee. Experience shows that such committees should be small if they are to be effective and not get trapped into becoming a bureaucratic machine.

In some organisations the Project Steering Committee is replaced by a Project Board. This often has wider powers, including approval of project plans, decisions on funding and budget approval and even initiation of projects up to a specified value. The responsibilities for each role will differ from one organisation to the next. Examples are given below:

The Project Sponsor

The Project Sponsor is likely to be a senior manager or executive who takes ownership of the project on behalf of the organisation. The level of this position depends on the appropriateness to the scope and anticipated cost of the project. The Sponsor has the responsibility for:

- Ensuring that the project meets the expectations of all the other stakeholders
- Ensuring that the project objectives are compatible with the organisation's strategy
- Demonstrating the organisation's commitment to the project through the resources made available
- Giving input to the project on strategic issues through an awareness of other activities continuing within the broader framework of the organisation

This role is essential where the project is likely to involve the organisation in major change or innovation, particularly where the results may have implications in other businesses in the group.

The Accountable Executive

As the name implies the Accountable Executive is the individual who is held to account for the success of the project, including the ultimate delivery of the planned benefits contained in the project objectives. Normally the role is filled by the most senior manager with an **active interest** in the project. This could be at group company, divisional or departmental level. It is not a full- time role but does involve the person appointed in maintaining a high enough level of involvement to ensure that the project is carefully planned, executed and controlled to defined standards.

The Accountable Executive does not get involved in the day to day management process which is the responsibility of the Project Leader.

The responsibilities of the role include:

- Ensure project objectives are compatible with organisational strategy
- Ensure the project remains viable throughout the life cycle
- Ensure the project is completed on time and within planned budget
- Appoint the Project Leader and be involved where appropriate in the selection (or approval) of the core members of the project team
- Establish critical success factors and their method of measurement
- Resolve any issues or conflicts brought forward by the Project Leader
- Maintain a close monitoring role on project costs either directly or through appointing a Financial Reviewer
- Monitor and control the project through regular progress reviews with the Project Leader
- Approve all plans and budgets and any subsequent changes made necessary by later inputs
- Submit regular progress reports to the Project Sponsor

- Arrange an independent health check on the project if ever needed
- Ensure the project stays on track to deliver the expected benefits

In some situations it is appropriate for the Sponsor and Accountable Executive to be the same individual. If the organisation has many projects running this is not desirable or practicable with projects spread over a wide range of functional areas of the business. It is important that the role has adequate authority to be effective in striving to satisfy the minimum obligations listed.

The Project Leader

Reporting directly to the Accountable Executive, as the Project Leader you manage the project on a day to day operational basis. Your appointment to this role is based on project management skills and experience rather than seniority or grade. Authority limits must be clearly defined and if the project is only part of your job, priorities should

be established and adjusted so that you can give adequate time to the project.

The responsibilities of your role include:

- Deliver the expected outcomes at each phase, on time and within budget
- Establish clear objectives, approved by the Accountable Executive
- Prepare all project plans and budgets, endorsed by the stakeholders
- Agree approval procedures for all plans
- Establish the project control system and measurement methods
- Report progress at regular, agreed intervals
- Monitor and track progress
- Resolve conflicts as they occur
- Maintain regular contact with all stakeholders
- Manage the team

These essential responsibilities can be combined with the key actions of the Action Cycle within the project life cycle to derive a Project Leader's checklist. This gives you a logical disciplined approach to effective and successful project management.

In some organisations two other components of the structure may exist:

- The Project Steering Committee
- The Financial Reviewer

The Project Steering Committee

When your project is large or makes demands across many functional boundaries, group companies or divisions,

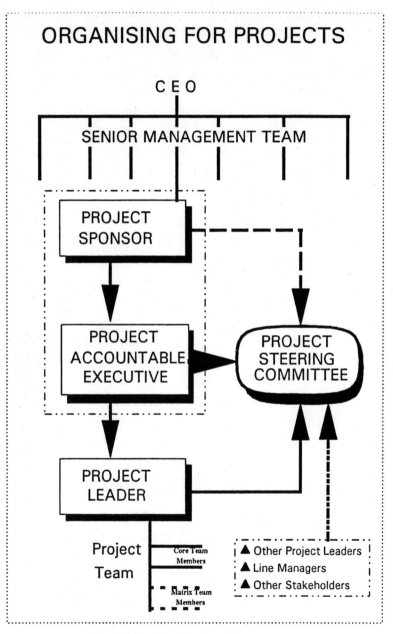

Fig. 7.1   The Project Structure

then you may have to work within the overall guidance of this body. Since the primary function is to provide direction and guidance, minimising conflicts across the boundaries, the committee can be very effective in taking decisions which are beyond the scope of control of the Accountable Executive. Membership is usually confined to a small number of key managers (6–8) or representatives with a high level of interest in the project. This could occasionally include other stakeholders such as the end user.

Where there are many projects running the committee is often a convenient way to keep line managers informed of progress on all projects and involve them in key decisions of a strategic nature. The chairperson is normally the Sponsor or Accountable Executive and you should always be present at meetings. Most organisations establish clear terms of reference and authority limits for the committee in its work. The meetings should be confined to the role of 'steering' and not reviewing your project progress. It may be helpful to coincide such meetings with major milestones or key stage completion points within your plan. This organisational structure is shown in Fig. 7.1.

The Financial Reviewer

Normally this role is filled by the Accountable Executive. The key responsibility of the role is to ensure the viability of your project is maintained at all stages. This is particularly true if you are forced by circumstances to modify your plans and some level of risk analysis is needed.

On large projects the role may be filled by a senior manager from the Finance Department.

THE TEAM

If the project organisational structure needs to be dynamic to meet the ever changing environment of the business, this naturally extends to the project team. For the flow of work associated with the project to proceed smoothly you must ensure that accountability, authority and responsibility is clearly defined for you and the individual members of the project team. The following definitions are used:

- ACCOUNTABILITY   being held totally answerable for the completion of allocated tasks to agreed standards of performance
- AUTHORITY   empowerment, i.e. the right granted to you to make and take decisions throughout the project
- RESPONSIBILITY   the obligation individuals feel to perform, effectively, the work of the project assigned to them to accepted standards of performance

Accountability is the total of authority and responsibility and part of this may be given to individual team members through the process of delegation. The accountability always remains with you as the project leader. Even when you have these three well defined, you need to establish good interface relationships with other line managers.

Few organisations can justify setting up a discrete project team with no other responsibilities except the one project. This is cost effective with large, long duration projects, but most are considerably smaller and the only cost effective structure is some form of matrix.

It is inevitable that some of your erstwhile colleagues will have an input to your project at some stage. This process takes up a great deal of time, particularly at the initial phase where a team structure is forming. It requires mutual trust between you and other managers who themselves are part of a team. But this project structure is different from the traditional line hierarchy that is familiar to everybody. You are asking other managers to work in an arrangement with which they may not feel comfortable – possibly because it means change.

In this arrangement many of the conflict problems arise from difficulties with authority, responsibility and accountability and their defined limits.

Traditional structure

The traditional line hierarchy defines a departmental structure based on functions where there is a concentration of particular technical expertise and experience. This is ideal for the project that does not require any expertise that is resident in a different functional area. The line manager in control of any function can maintain budget control, establish new budgets and have them approved by senior management. Authority and responsibility are usually well defined, communication and feedback channels are established on a personal level in the confined internal environment of the department and its own culture.

Other internal advantages of the functional structure are:

- Flexibility of resources
- Easier prioritisation of workloads
- Effective technical control
- Effective teamworking established

- Easier control of costs
- Communication vertically is established
- Reacts quickly to crisis

There are disadvantages to this approach, the most obvious being there is no clear Sponsor or Accountable Executive. There could be many projects in progress in the organisation at the same time with no central authority ensuring these are being directed within the context of corporate strategy. Customer focus is often missing and when activities in the project dictate the need to cross functional lines, conflicts occur and project delays are likely to result. Cultural differences between departments are created by the line managers and these can generate conflicts over standards of working, work practices and efficiency. It is unavoidable that managers will tend to prioritise tasks that provide benefits to themselves and their team. Problems are sent up the line for senior management decisions which are slow in coming, leading to frustration, particularly where a committee is involved.

To complete a project successfully and meet objectives requires the effective use of available resources, working to high standards. This is extremely difficult across functions without the regular involvement of senior management who often believe they have better things to do.

The matrix structure

The matrix organisation is a way of combining the advantages of the functional structure into a flexible arrangement similar to a product grouping. You and your colleague project leaders report to a senior manager or director, each project becoming a budget centre in its own right, with accountability vested in each project leader.

For the matrix approach to work, authority and accountability for project success is solely in your hands. Your colleague functional managers have the responsibility to maintain excellence of their departmental inputs to your project. This leads to a need for clear definitions of your limits of authority and prompt handling of any conflict between functional areas. Good and effective communication is obligatory across all functional interfaces if you are to succeed in getting open commitment of resources and ongoing support. It is important for you to ensure there is no doubt about where accountability is vested and that there are no erroneous perceptions of dual accountability in the team or among your colleagues and senior managers. Some advantages of the matrix structure are:

- Better resource control through line managers
- Rapid response to conflict, problems and changes in the project's interests
- Procedures and systems can be customised to the project needs as long as they do not openly conflict with standing orders.
- Priorities can be negotiated and commitments agreed
- Better use of appropriate skills for project
- More cost effective when several projects are active
- Promotes skills development in people to meet needs
- Less stress from shared responsibility with functional line managers

This does not mean there are no disadvantages, because there are several. One common problem is repetitive reporting from two or more points in the matrix and

The traditional Line Structure

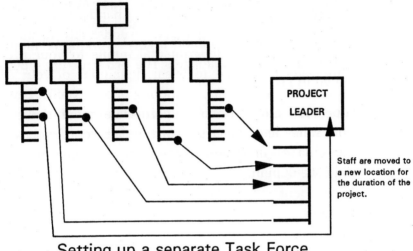

Setting up a separate Task Force

The Matrix Structure

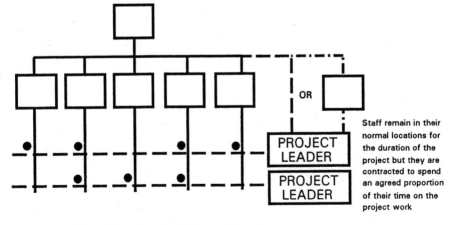

Fig. 7.2   Project Team Structure

you must take action to minimise the wasted effort on this activity. The other primary difficulty experienced by most project leaders is the changes in priorities which occur without you being kept informed. This can lead to power struggles and you can minimise such problems by taking some positive steps to build a good working relationship with your colleague managers. The two structure types are shown in Fig. 7.2.

There are many possible permutations of these two approaches and the best structure for your organisation and situation must be derived by participative discussion and consultation.

Summary

- *Project management involves organisational interfacing at all levels*
- *An organisational structure for projects is essential to project success*
- *There are three levels of the structure:*
    - *the SPONSOR at the strategic level*
    - *the ACCOUNTABLE EXECUTIVE at senior level with full authority*
    - *the PROJECT LEADER responsible for the day to day work*
- *A PROJECT STEERING COMMITTEE provides direction and guidance for projects*
- *The project team structure must be clearly defined, particularly with a matrix*

8

Managing the Outside

At the earliest possible stages of the project inception you used the project window to identify the known stakeholders – all those people, clients, end users, suppliers, consultants and yourself who have an interest in the project. More specifically this group has an interest in the final outcome but some will also have a vested interest in the process aspects of your management. What you do with the team and how the work is done is more of interest to some stakeholders than others. The impact on all of them of decisions you take in the interests of the project must be given due consideration within the wider picture of the outside.

This presents you and your management with an additional challenge. Decisions you take have a direct impact on

those stakeholders over whom you have authority. Those decisions also have an impact on those stakeholders over whom you do not have any authority. Yet this group can have a significant influence on your progress towards the stated objectives, even by direct intervention on certain occasions!

Stakeholder management is an accepted part of the successful strategic management of any business, so there is no reason not to apply similar principles to your project. Clearly the effective management of your project process is not possible without considering these outside influences at the earliest possible stage. This means you must take a pro-active role to reduce the possibility of the potential adverse effects of stakeholder activities. This has the benefit of giving the project team more opportunities to encourage support from the stakeholders, keeping them both involved and informed.

Stakeholder Management

If you fail to recognise, or co-operate with, one or more of your project stakeholders, then you risk hindering a successful outcome, even failing to achieve your project objectives. Indeed, it only needs one such stakeholder to force their particular views on to you at a time that is least convenient to your project, to destabilise your efforts. You are the project leader and this allows you to set the ground rules from the start. This is essential if you are to maintain control and build a well motivated, successful team.

Many of the stakeholders to a project were identified in Fig. 4.2 but to manage this group you must take the process of identification further:

- Identify stakeholders as two groups
  INTERNAL
  EXTERNAL
- Gather information about each
- Identify their objectives – visible and invisible
- Determine their strengths and weaknesses
- Predict their behaviour and motivation
- Establish how the project fits in their strategy

You are normally in a better position to seek and obtain the information on these elements with the group of Internal or **key stakeholders**, because most will be readily accessible and known to you. Moreover they will generally have clear vested interests in supporting you as they form an integral part of the project team. You must ensure you use this support wherever possible to develop a project strategy of which the group can also share ownership. In your role as project leader you will have defined your authority with the Sponsor and clearly this authority should extend over the group of inner stakeholders. Remember this authority extends only over the project, since some inner stakeholders are likely to hold a more senior position in the line hierarchy.

However, you may need to include within this group one or more stakeholders who are not inside the organisation. The end user or customer could be an outsider to the organisation, but they may still need to be included in the 'internal' or key stakeholder group to retain their close involvement with the project as it proceeds.

What benefits can you expect?

Gathering the data about stakeholders is not always an easy task, but you have several benefits to gain from the activity. These will help you to maintain control of the project process and benefit the team in executing the work, particularly where there are interfaces on a frequent basis with certain stakeholders. With reference to all the stakeholders, this will help you and your team to:

- Understand corporate and strategic relevance of the project to them
- Appreciate any economic interests in the final outcomes
- Be fully aware of any legal rights they have
- Assess the political dimension and its relevance
- Raise awareness of any Health and Safety issues relevant in the implementation stage
- Define preferred methods of contact, when and with whom
- Establish jointly agreed working arrangements for the project at every phase

■ Appreciate the external influences on them and their business which could influence their behaviour

Through establishing these benefits you should now be in a position to make a judgement on the 'value' each stakeholder is putting on their involvement in the project. This helps to assess how much potential influence each will try to exert on the project and its outcome.

With your project team, draw up a table of the stakeholders, ranked in order of the valuations as shown in Fig. 8.1. Then identify the key stages of the project in which each stakeholder has an interest by giving them a ranking of 'HIGH', 'MEDIUM', or 'LOW'.

The completed table gives you an overview and complete picture of which stakeholders need to be 'managed' by the team throughout each of the key stages of the project. If appropriate allocate this managing role for each stakeholder to a specific team member. This allocation of responsibility

NO.	STAKEHOLDER	I/O	PROJECT KEY STAGE																	
			1	2	3	4	5	6	7	8	9	10	11	12	13	14	15	16	17	18
1																				
2																				
3																				
4																				
5																				
6																				
7																				
8																				
9																				
10																				

KEY: I:Inner, O:Outer, H:High, M:Medium, L:Low

Fig. 8.1 Summary of stakeholder valuations

must not conflict with the lines of accountability you have defined for the project team. The management of the most important key stakeholders must remain your responsibility.

Although you prepare this list of stakeholders at the outset, do not accept that it is frozen. The list will almost certainly change as the project progresses through the life cycle. Make it a point to review the list and the valuation rankings at every project review meeting. Add new stakeholders and remove those whose interest and involvement has ceased irrevocably.

Actions you can take

Constructing a summary of stakeholder's interests is an essential part of your strategy for managing the outside of the project. But the inner workings of the project process are closely integrated with everything that happens with this group. In practice the involvement of the key stakeholders is almost continuous as a group. Other stakeholders may have a limited involvement and only at specific stages of the work. So the external stakeholder group membership tends to change with time as the project proceeds.

The Action Cycle (see Section 5) includes specific actions you take to achieve your objectives. This was integrated into the project life cycle which includes the stakeholders. This gives a convenient framework from which to derive the **'key actions'** you need to take to ensure your leadership of the project is effective.

STEP 1

Defining the objectives and deadlines

Your initial task is to identify clearly the project purpose and ensure that all stakeholders are in accord with this statement. Without this clear understanding from the outset you will not find it easy to define the project objectives. It is obviously intrinsic to purpose that the benefits of the project for the organisation are identified. This must also be agreed by the stakeholders even though some will almost certainly have their own benefits they hope to gain from a successful outcome of the project.

At this stage you need to establish how and where the project fits in to the organisational strategy. This is not always so easy since the context may involve some longer term plans that for numerous reasons cannot be exposed to you. However you are faced with convincing others that the project has a high value to help generate enthusiasm and commitment, so try to set the project in a justifiable context.

The key stakeholders will probably have been identified but you should check that the list of interested people, departments or divisions is complete. Identification of the external stakeholders will not be comprehensive at this stage since some will only appear after the start of planning or even later. Finally you must establish the project priorities within the framework of corporate activities and priorities. If the project is successful in giving the expected outcomes when are these needed by the organisation? Ask; "What are the consequences of late delivery of the results?" Decide the deadline for completion and include some contingency to allow for the unknown events which inevitably will interfere with your plans and schedules.

STEP 2

Prepare project plans and briefing

The planning process is concerned initially with gathering information. You have an opportunity now to dig a little deeper and find out more about the needs and expectations of the stakeholders. Determine the individual and personal objectives and where possible find out the underlying reasons for their current thinking. Explore if the project is derived from earlier problems and whether attempts have been made previously to find an acceptable solution. If this has happened find out as much as possible about their previous experiences, good and bad.

Many of the inner stakeholders may have functional roles in the project execution. Just what part they will play needs to be established in principle at this stage, before you get into detailed planning. The end user will be one of your main contacts throughout the project. This may be one person or a committee, but you must establish a good working understanding with them. Derive a project specification if this is possible or feasible at this stage. Define the scope of the work and agree what is definitely not required. This is a continuing process throughout the project as part of your regular reviews with the stakeholders.

Planning involves laying out a structure for the project team and, if necessary, the organisation as far as your project is concerned (see Section 7). Inform the stakeholders and agree with them where they fit in this structure and reporting procedures you intend to adopt. Also ensure you include lateral communication across functional boundaries in your communication procedures and that stakeholders understand the importance of this channel.

Once the planning process is complete you must share your commitment with the stakeholders and seek their endorsement of all your plans. The amount of detail you expose will depend on the importance of any stakeholder in the group. The Accountable Executive will obviously expect to see more than a functional manager who has an interest in one particular part. The latter then needs to see and understand the detail of that part which affects or involves them.

As the most important key stakeholder the Accountable Executive should sign off all plans as approved for execution. Other stakeholders should sign off and approve as you decide is necessary to ensure their commitment to the role they must play to ensure you can fulfil your responsibilities in the project. This approval process also makes sure that all stakeholders do understand their responsibilities in the project and just what they are committing themselves or their departments to do for you. This may only involve provision of resources and the prioritisation of their availability, but this is a vital commitment for you to implement the project.

STEP 3

Implement, monitor and track the Project

The implementation of the project is not always something that has a clear 'lift-off' date. Although it might seem tidier to do this, in practice some work often has to start before planning is complete. You may have to do this to gather further data for the next level of planning to proceed for a later stage of execution. This is often true with 'soft' projects where there are many unknowns at the early stages.

Since all your plans have been agreed, accepted and approved by the stakeholders the project execution can proceed with the systems and procedures you have established. These will keep them informed of progress and through use of the list you derived in Fig. 8.1 you can ensure that every stakeholder is kept in close contact with at least one nominated member of the project team. All progress reports must be signed off as accepted and if any of your plans are modified to resolve unexpected problems then approval procedures must be followed.

During execution conflicts between departments and stakeholders are almost inevitable. In the interests of the project you must take prompt action to resolve these as rapidly as possible. If necessary invoke the assistance of the Accountable Executive or even, on occasions, the Project Sponsor.

STEP 4

Project run-down and evaluation

The project run-down phase is where you have the opportunity to tidy up the loose ends and ensure that the project can move smoothly into a handover to the end user. You must check that all stakeholder expectations have been satisfied and that the expected benefits have been realised. You must identify and record any shortcomings from the objectives with reasons why the initial outcomes have not been achieved. At the same time identify any additional beneficial outcomes that have occurred either during the execution or as a result of the final results.

Few projects come to a clean and tidy end on a specific day. There are often follow on activities and maintenance tasks to be set up and these may require your input on a part-time basis for several weeks or months. You need to identify all these possible activities, who is responsible for them being carried out and the communication procedures needed to ensure rapid reaction to any problems occurring. Some stakeholders may have a continuing involvement in these activities so you must ensure they understand and accept their responsibilities.

This is an opportunity to identify any key learning points which came out of the work of your project which could help further projects in the organisation. This evaluation can cover all aspects of the project through the four phases of the life cycle. It is valuable to record the results of this evaluation in a final Project Report which should be signed off as accepted by the key stakeholders.

Summary

- *Identify the stakeholders – both the INTERNAL and EXTERNAL*
- *Understand the stakeholders motives, objectives, strengths, weaknesses, strategy*
- *Value stakeholders and assign responsibilities for contact and management*
- *Identify the actions you must take with each stakeholder group throughout the LIFE CYCLE*
- *Ensure the team members understand their roles with respect to stakeholders*
- *Derive clearly understood procedures for stakeholder agreement, approvals, sign-offs*

9 Managing the Inside

If you are to maintain your focus on the project objectives you are constantly trying to ensure that the team is working well together and individuals in the team have all the necessary information and skills to do the work. This presumes that sufficiently detailed plans are prepared and all procedures, working practices and controls are agreed and operating.

The leadership model derived earlier (see Section 6) showed that to achieve the project objectives you must give attention to the three principal areas of your role:

- Achieving project tasks and deadlines
- Build and maintain the team
- Develop team member appropriate skills

The ideal situation is to hold these three areas in balance, giving an appropriate amount of your time to each as the need arises. It is almost certain that you regard yourself as one of the team – or at least your manager does! So part of the work you will execute, since you were probably selected for the leadership job because of the experience and skills you can bring to the project. As a 'working team leader' you have this dual function, yet it is important to get your leadership role in true perspective. You should not attempt to take the greater part of the work on to your desk, or even the more interesting parts. Ensure that by assigning and where necessary delegating, others carry the load to allow you time to fulfil the obligations of the leadership role.

It is inevitable that as the project moves forward you will find yourself at times spending more time in one area than another. This is essential to effective leadership as you give particular attention to either the task area, the team or assisting and guiding individual team members. Remember that you have stakeholders to manage also and you must take the overview position at regular intervals to see the full picture developing. This really means you must take a break from what you are doing and step away from your own personal track at the time to check what is happening elsewhere in all the areas.

Your monitoring will keep you informed and ensure that problems are not developing without them being given prompt attention. It also makes sure you do not become strongly focused on one particular area for too long and lose sight of what is going on in other directions. You can liken this to piloting your own helicopter – taking a quick flight round the 'estate', looking down from above to check that all is well with the project.

Managing the inside requires you to exercise control of these three areas and places high demands on your skill as a leader. Leading is all about action and in each of these areas there are many actions you need to take on a repetitive basis throughout the project. Some you may take only occasionally, depending which phase of the project you are in, but the Action Cycle is a reiterative and dynamic process which involves you in continuous review.

Remember that effective leadership is all about **what you do** not what you are. This is not to say the skills and abilities you have are unimportant, on the contrary they must be relevant to the work of the project, but how you use them is the key to your success.

The Action Cycle (see Chapter 5) includes the actions you must take in each area at each step of the cycle if you are to achieve your objectives. This can help you to derive a list of **'key actions'** you need to take to ensure your leadership is effective.

Achieving project tasks and deadlines

STEP 1

Defining the objectives and deadlines

You need to be clear in your own mind from the outset what it is you are expected to achieve by establishing the project purpose and its scope. You must identify the constraints on both the scope and the way you are expected to operate. These constraints may be people oriented or involve time, money, materials or equipment.

You must then satisfy yourself that you believe you can achieve the objectives within the limits set by these constraints. If not then you may have to negotiate some new ground rules at the outset. It is not to your credit to try to manage 'project impossible' just to prove that someone else was wrong. All you succeed in doing is wasting money and effort and maybe embarrass somebody. Clarify your terms of reference before you start work and establish a working relationship with your Accountable Executive or Sponsor.

STEP 2

Prepare project plans and briefing

At the outset you may be presented with a feasibility report and your first concern is to satisfy yourself its contents are still valid and true. If there are doubts about the budgets, costings, timings or conclusions then you must dispel them before proceeding. You will then start the planning process, assisted by the team you have selected or been allocated. This may be just a small core team at this stage, but you will derive a more effective plan eventually if you involve the team in the planning process. You will identify the Key Stages of the plan and start to identify all the project activities. Where you find alternative approaches or methods you will weigh these with your team and make a decision. You then establish all the activity' dependencies, decide on milestones and deadlines and draw the plan into a presentable form.

This requires you to decide which planning tools are appropriate to use for the project. If considered necessary, produce a network diagram and Gantt charts then analyse the resource needs. Based on these plans you are able to identify a major part of the resource needs for the project, including the finance and budgets. You must then start the process of finding the resources you need, which usually means people to do the work.

If you are not successful or find you have additional constraints of time, then you will need to review and modify your plans before seeking stakeholder approval.

After setting up agreed schedules you may have to set performance standards within the framework of existing quality standards. You will then ensure through briefing that everyone understands the plan and all the schedules, work breakdown details and the procedures and methods of control you propose to use. At this more advanced stage you can also clarify the objectives (particularly if some changes have occurred during planning), purpose and scope of the project. You will finally seek stakeholder approval and sign off your plans before implementation.

STEP 3

Implement, monitor and track the Project

To implement the project you must identify the cross-functional barriers which you must cross to ensure that the work is carried out on time. You will use your influence and authority to ensure you receive the right skills you need from each department or functional area in the organisation.

A key element of your role is to organise the project and issue the work breakdowns and work plans for individuals in each department along with the relevant responsibility charts and budget sheets. This is a progressive activity as the work of the project proceeds. You will monitor the progress regularly, making and taking decisions where and when necessary to modify plans and seek stakeholder agreement and approval for such changes.

You regularly review progress against the original or *'base plan'* and agree action plans to deal with problems and difficulties and highlighted variances. You monitor to ensure performance standards are maintained and as each work plan is finished to your satisfaction, it is signed off as complete.

STEP 4

Project run-down and evaluation

As the project proceeds you report progress against the base plan, giving explanation of any variances, positive and negative. Regular summaries of the state of the project in all its various facets keeps the stakeholders informed and helps maintain senior management support. You maintain a review of the project objectives to ensure there have been no diversions or changes. If progress is not going well you may need to consult stakeholders and the team to establish what the problems are and why they have occurred. This analysis will help you to decide upon corrective action.

In some projects it may be necessary to set up sub-projects for the subsequent implementation of the project outcomes. This could involve other departments which have not been involved up to this point. This might be a production department which could start planning new production facilities or training of operatives in preparation for the completion of your project. This *'concurrent implementation'* is a common feature for different parts of the project in order to reduce the time for final implementation of all the outcomes of the project. The sub-projects will probably have their own project leader from the newly involved department and you then have a further co-ordination activity. You can assign this activity to one of your team members, preferably one who has carried out the work to date.

As the project approaches a final completion date you may have several such sub-projects still active. In addition you can set up a small team for follow on and maintenance activities to support the end users, provide a trouble-shooting service and give assistance and training where necessary. Finally you will compile manuals where appropriate and prepare your final evaluation report.

Build and maintain the team
Develop team member appropriate skills

STEP 1

Defining the objectives and deadlines

When the project core team comes together and the team members are identified you will need to have your first team meeting. Your purpose here is to explain the background to the project, expose the project objectives and generally share your own commitment to the work ahead. This is a critical activity for you at this stage as you are the organisation's sales person, your goal being to influence the new team to take on ownership of the project.

You are able to explain the scope of the project and clarify some of their concerns which might appear at this early stage. It is important at this point to ensure each team member is clear about the objectives so that they can individually assess the contribution they could make to the project. You need this step to start creating the right climate in the team, allowing each team member to come to terms with the contribution that they will be asked to make and match this with their own valuation of their ability to satisfy the project needs. This will lead to acceptance and upon this you can build commitment. Your enthusiasm is infectious to the team and will make a significant contribution to good teamwork during the project.

STEP 2

Prepare project plans and briefing

At the start of the project, as the team starts working together, it is important for you to involve them as much as possible in gathering data and previous experience. They will have useful contributions to make and as a group of individuals have a fund of creative ideas and suggestions you can tap into. You consult them by asking open questions to find out as much as possible that can help the project planning process. Do not expose your ideas first as they may come up with some better ones which can be adapted. This process is giving you an opportunity to start building the team and use the team synergy to good effect. It also gives you an opportunity to observe and assess the skills of your team members and start to identify development needs for the project work.

As you enter the true planning stage you involve the team members in identifying the activities to be carried out and their inter-dependencies, using the skills and past experience of the individuals. You take any essential decisions necessary to structure the team for parts of the project and identify the work plans. You derive the responsibility charts and assign the work plans based on your structure and assessment of individual skills or to other departments.

At this stage it is appropriate to start having regular 1:1 discussions with team members, based on a four weekly cycle. You use these opportunities to get to know and understand each member of the team, their likes and dislikes, skills and preferences and explore development needs and opportunities. You agree performance targets with each team member to help you maintain high standards of teamworking and resolve any problems and difficulties which are interfering with performance. If you are delegating some of your authority you must follow a careful process of coaching to ensure the individual team member accepts the additional responsibility.

Regular briefings are not to be confused with progress review meetings. It may be useful to have a short briefing meeting once a week, for example on a Monday morning. Here you can explain decisions and check the team's understanding, respond to questions and listen to their views as you consult them. It allows you to check that there are no anticipated problems with the work to be carried out in the week ahead and if there are some already known, decide what actions are necessary. Throughout, it is important to maintain your own enthusiasm and commitment to the team and for the project.

STEP 3

Implement, monitor and track the project

Your principal concern during this step is to co-ordinate the team's efforts and ensure the work is progressing to plan without any problems or conflicts. You must act promptly to resolve such problems to keep the team focused on its deadlines. If there are resource conflicts these must also be resolved, although as the teamwork develops many of these problems will be resolved by self-help from within the team. Where necessary you get involved as the problems surface at the regular progress meetings that you have marked into the project plan.

You use every opportunity to coach and advise individual team members to develop their skills, particularly in problem-solving, and review performance at the regular meetings. You review performance and encourage improvements where you can see the scope after discussion. You must ensure standards are maintained and a strong sense of discipline is generated in the team. Remember to give praise and recognition when it is merited – a few words of praise and open recognition of people's efforts are motivating and help create respect and trust between you and the team. Be

seen to champion the interests of your team and support them openly when necessary.

Check regularly , by 'walking the job', that communications are working well and regular reports are reaching you. Be seen to check and verify these reports personally but be careful not to peer 'over the shoulder'. Show that you are keen to help whatever the problem and even seek help from elsewhere. You will also discover if anyone is over- or under-loaded at any time, particularly in a matrix situation where other work may be given priority without you being told.

STEP 4

Project run-down and termination

Use the team meetings and briefings to review performance, including yourself. Agree steps to take to improve things as needed and take actions you have agreed. Do not make promises you cannot or do not intend to fulfil. Evaluate cross-functional working and the interfaces and take action if there are problems developing by alerting the problem to your colleague managers in other departments. Give recognition as appropriate and let others know about outstanding performance.

As each work plan is completed and signed off, ensure you evaluate the performance and keep the momentum of the project going at the right pace to meet the deadlines. If there are clear learning points that come out of a particular piece of work, ensure these are recorded and tell the team about them. Get the team member who carried out the work to give a short presentation to everyone so they can all learn from the experience.

Most people are alert to opportunities for personal gain and if you know your team you will soon be aware of team members' personal motives. Where you can, take steps to reward high performance on the project either during or at the end of the project. Identify any training needs that show up and take action to satisfy these when you can within the constraints of the project schedules.

Summarising

As with your role in 'managing the outside', there are many actions you take in 'managing the inside' of the project in order to achieve the project objectives. Many of these are repeated countless times, some even on a daily basis as the action cycle is a dynamic process. You may find others which are appropriate to your project, but whatever you do it must be directed towards maintaining the overall focus on objectives. Project leadership is not a conductor role, but involves drive, effort, belief and a strong desire to achieve success.

Everyone has their own style of leading a team, and to get results you need to achieve a balance between the needs and expectations of the stakeholders and maintaining a minimum level of morale in the team to get acceptable performance.

Summary

- *Maintain a balance between the three functional areas*
- *When you get involved remember to stand back occasionally – take a helicopter view*

- *Identify the key actions you must take at each phase of the LIFE CYCLE*
- *Evaluate performance as a continuous process*
- *Pay attention to the team's needs – maintain motivation at a high level*
- *Maintain overall focus on project objectives*

10

The Project Leader's Checklist

Having reached this far in the book you are either secretly overjoyed to find you have been doing it right all along or you are having serious doubts about your future! Yes, there are a great many things you have to think about when leading a project, especially as most of the time you are under the stress of continual pressure of priorities of both the project and your other work. It takes all your concentration to feel you are on top of the job and maintain an appearance of cool, calm confidence that you really are in control.

You will need all your skills of organisation and time management to effectively organise the project and the team to ensure priorities are correctly assessed at all times. It is helpful to keep a Project Diary in the form of an A4, hard cover notebook. Carry this at all times and start a fresh page each day. *Record everything that happens and that you do*. Notes from meetings, 1:1 discussions, telephone conversations and external contacts should be recorded along with reminders and thoughts for future reference. Make checklists for short term priorities and items for weekly briefings.

In the previous sections the Key Actions you take have been identified as the project moves through the four phases of the project life cycle. These actions can be used to compile the essential elements of a checklist for project leadership. This can be done for both the Inner and Outer directed modes of the leadership model developed in Section 5.

These two checklists are shown in Fig. 10.1 and Fig. 10.2. Remember these are limited to the essential elements and you can add other actions you have to take on your projects to focus the list to your own needs. Organisational requirements may dictate certain actions you have to take that are specific to the industry or type of project. The purpose of the checklist is to give you a starting point as the basis of developing one relevant to your situation. It is an effective way to monitor yourself and you can keep people informed of the agreed priorities for action. In some situations you can issue such checklists to people or write them up on a flip chart – the public exposure ensures people are informed and have no excuses for not receiving information.

The actions you take are all directed towards the achievement of the project objectives and you may have not been consulted in the preparation of these. However, it is important that you understand and accept them as stated

KEY ACTIONS - OUTER DIRECTED			
THE STAKEHOLDERS			
CONCEPTION	DEFINE OBJECTIVES & DEADLINES		Identify Project purpose & deadlines Authority and accountability Organizational benefits Project context in Corporate strategy Establish corporate priorities Identify all stakeholders
PLANNING	PREPARE PROJECT PLANS & BRIEF EVERYBODY	GATHER DATA	Establish needs & expectations Identify functional roles & inputs Establish end user specifications
		TAKE DECISIONS	Project structure/methodology Agree reporting procedures Establish project priorities Inter-functional communication
		BRIEFING	Clarify stakeholder responsibilities Endorse & approve plans Share commitment Clarify resource priorities
EXECUTION	IMPLEMENT MONITOR & TRACK THE PROJECT		Gain acceptance of plans Resolve inter-functional conflicts Maintain stakeholders commitment Sign off progress reports Involve stakeholders in replanning
TERMINATION	PROJECT / TASK RUNDOWN & EVALUATION		Review progress & objectives Stakeholder approval of changes Stakeholders expectations Evaluate objectives against results Additional benefits Follow-on/maintenance /service contacts

Fig. 10.1   Project Leader's Key Actions – Outer directed

KEY ACTIONS - INNER DIRECTED

LIFE-CYCLE PHASE		ACHIEVE PROJECT TASKS AND DEADLINES	BUILD AND MAINTAIN THE TEAM	DEVELOP TEAM MEMBER APPROPRIATE SKILLS
CONCEPTION	DEFINE OBJECTIVES & DEADLINES	Establish project purpose/scope Agree project objectives Identify resource constraints Identify operating constraints	Identify core team Hold team meeting Describe project objectives Share your commitment	Clarify objectives Gain acceptance
PLANNING	PREPARE PROJECT PLANS & BRIEF EVERYBODY — GATHER DATA	Check feasibility report Review resource needs Establish options Identify key stages	Involve team in planning Discover past experience Consult team for ideas & suggestions Assess and develop individual skills	
	TAKE DECISIONS	Decide planning tools Identify activities Determine dependencies Establish schedules Decide deadlines/milestones	Structure the team as necessary Establish the work breakdown structure Design the work packages/plans Determine individual responsibilities Assign work packages/plans	Delegate Agree targets Set meetings schedule Establish reporting procedures
	BRIEFING	Set standards / QA Clarify objectives Explain plan Describe control systems	Set up briefings schedule Identify short term priorities Listen to team's views Check understanding	Explain all decisions Ask open questions & respond Maintain enthusiasm & commitment
EXECUTION	IMPLEMENT MONITOR & TRACK THE PROJECT	Identify cross-functional interfaces Agree resource availability Organise work plans Review progress Track against base plan Maintain standards Sign off completed packages	Co-ordinate teamworking Identify problems Agree action plans Resolve conflicts Resolve resource constraints Support team efforts	Give guidance as needed Advise and coach new skills Review performance Encourage and assist Stress priorities Recognise effort
TERMINATION	PROJECT / TASK RUNDOWN & EVALUATION	Report progress Identify variances and action plans Review objectives Replan as necessary Establish sub-projects if needed Follow-on/maintenance/service Review your leadership	Review team performance Evaluate cross-functional working Reconcile cross-functional conflicts Identify valuable learning points Give team recognition	Appraise performance Review targets Give praise & reward Identify further training needs

Fig. 10.2 Project Leader's Key Actions – Inner directed

when you are appointed to lead the project. If necessary, review the prepared statements to ensure they are as comprehensive as possible, although this is usually more difficult for the soft project. Some guidelines for setting objectives are given in Chapter 12.

Summary

- *Keep a Project Diary yourself*
- *Record everything that happens*
- *Use the Leader's checklists – add more actions or delete some as appropriate*
- *Derive specific checklists for action for the team and/or other departments*

11 Steps to Success

What constitutes success? Why are some projects perceived by some as failures, particularly when they are perceived as:

- Finishing on schedule
- Finishing within the project budget
- Meeting all core objectives
- Meeting all stakeholders' expectations?

Conversely some projects are perceived as successful even when they fail to meet the first two of these factors. Project success, like beauty in art, is all in the perception of the observer. Everybody sees different elements of the project as successful, so measurement of success is subjective according to what an individual gains from the work.

If measurement is objective then success is directly related to:

- **Achieving project objectives**
- **Meeting all stakeholder expectations**
- **Meeting project team expectations**

A high level of satisfaction among everyone involved with the project and all those affected by the outcomes is perceived as a measure of success. Time and cost are necessarily included in the objectives of the project. If either or both of these exceed plans other outcomes measured as successful are given high profile, sometimes to compensate for the partial failure! Of course in this type of situation it is important that in the euphoria of 'success', the project team does not lose the opportunity to establish why the over-runs occurred and learn from the analysis.

Achieving success is directly related to the effort made by the leader and the team to identify the potential difficulties and take appropriate steps to minimise or avoid them in practice. The project leader needs good forecasting skills among many others to ensure the project team has genuine satisfaction from a successful outcome.

Predicting Success

Predicting whether a project will be successful is one of the most difficult tasks. If the measurement is based on time, cost and identified performance parameters, it is relatively easy to establish contributions to profits directly or through improved efficiency. But does this constitute success in terms of the way the project was managed? As success is clearly measured by people's perceptions, you can only truly determine your success by the actions you have taken at every stage and their outcomes. The extent to which these actions have contributed to your success are less obvious to others. You and your team will be only too aware of the actions that you take which directly stimulate success. As a minimum these will include:

- Select the team members yourself
- Select appropriate skills and proven experience
- Share your commitment from the outset
- Establish your authority at the outset
- Co-ordinate the stakeholders' involvement
- Involve the team in decision making and taking
- Involve the team in problem solving
- Involve the team in planning and scheduling
- Ensure you use appropriate planning tools
- Maintain project objectives in high profile
- Maintain senior management support throughout
- Ensure project organisation is accepted by everyone
- Accept the need for flexibility from the start
- Establish and maintain effective communication procedures
- Establish and maintain effective control procedures

All these process factors contribute to your success irrespective of the type of project or its duration. In addition there are other essential factors for success which are objectives based for your specific project. These may be derived from the outcomes or consequences of the work of the project or based on some direct measurement of particular parameters. It is important that these success criteria are established at the outset so that the degree of success can eventually be judged.

What Affects Success?

The path to success is littered with difficulties at every stage. Many of these occur due to insufficient attention to detail and failure to anticipate problems. The factors which can interfere or prevent project success are listed under six headings:

- The project base
- The planning of the project
- The organisation and control of the project
- Monitoring and tracking progress
- The stakeholders
- The Project Leader and team performance

It is no coincidence that this list is a combination of the four phases of a project life cycle and the three dimensions of your role as project leader.

The project base

Like the foundations of any structure, the project base must be soundly constructed with a maximum acceptable level of defects. The project structure within the organisation must be clearly identified indicating which senior manager is accountable for your project. A Project Board or Steering Committee is a convenient way of ensuring all projects are following a direction in line with corporate strategy and current business plans. This will also ensure commitment and support is maintained at the highest level and if business strategy is changed due to external pressures, decisions about ongoing projects can be rapidly taken. If this does not exist you must work to ensure you have a clear understanding yourself of the project context. Possible difficulties you could encounter include:

- Organisation prefers stability, lacking strategic change
- New 'type' of project

- Inability to assess risk
- Lack of clear interfaces in organisation
- Unclear structure for decision taking
- Poor project definition – vague objectives
- Deficient problem solving skills
- Scope of the project not defined
- Lack of project management skills

The presence of these factors will contribute to failure. Lack of essential skills will leave the project attempting to start with key ingredients absent. These, combined with poor management support will leave you with an impossible choice. Stay with the project out of loyalty and belief (and possibly hope) or take a fast track out in consideration of your career!

Poor results or perceived failure nearly always reflect on you, the project leader, even if they are due to factors and situations beyond your direct control.

Planning the project

The most serious error made repeatedly by many managers, particularly at senior levels, is the belief that planning is something that just happens as the project progresses. Flexibility of approach is claimed to be the underlying reason for this misguided view. Failing to plan adequately is the surest way to plan failure. If you have led a project before, you will now know from bitter experience that planning is not about doing next what seems to be right and then later finding some important tasks have been omitted. This leads to a project in permanent crisis and is almost certain to fail to meet objectives. Possible difficulties include:

- Lack of time allowed
- Lack of planning skills
- Planning at one level
- Planning tools selected too complex
- Poor estimating
- Lack of team involvement and consultation
- Poor assessment of resources, competence and capacity
- Poor communication procedures and skills
- Unsuitable climate for creativity in planning
- Lack of clear milestones and deadlines
- Inability to handle conflicts effectively

Planning is most effective when done as a participative activity with all the team members involved – or at least those appointed at this point. If the team is allowed to contribute then acceptance and commitment is generated. Ownership which starts at the conceptual stage is reinforced and this makes a major contribution to the project's eventual success.

Organisation and control of the project

The problem which seems to face most organisations when a new project is conceived is its inability to define clearly your authority and responsibilities. It is obvious that this failing is regenerative because the team also suffers from the same problem from the beginning. A lack of any basic guidelines for a project control system is another major difficulty. Others include:

- Lack of clear project structure
- Inadequate detail in the plans
- Confused scheduling
- Inability to work in a matrix structure
- Poor co-ordination with all levels

- Key resources not available according to plans
- Poor prioritising
- Unclear responsibilities of team members
- Insufficient Leader influence
- Lack of customised administrative systems for the project
- Progress meetings not planned in advance
- No agreed reporting procedures and methods
- Measurement procedures not established
- Poor performance data collection, recording and analysis

Good administrative skills and attention to detail are essential if you are to maintain the momentum of your project. These will help to anticipate problems that can endanger the project plan and support problem solving by involving the team when it is necessary. Superb plans with the fullest detail are of little value at the implementation phase, if your control and organisation is defective and ineffective.

Monitoring and tracking the project

It is easy to imagine your project will have a planned implementation date when the starting gun goes off and everyone rushes into a frenzy of activity. The reality is quite different and failure to recognise the importance of a phased start that is co-ordinated with the planning activity can lead you and the team to many problems and confusion. You can, of course, sit back at your desk and wait for all the progress and status reports to land in your in- tray. The only problem is that nothing happens! Fail to monitor effectively and you will not be in control or be in a position to track the project against the base plan. Other difficulties include:

- Unclear work plans
- Unclear reporting procedures

- Little contact with team members
- Little or no contact with stakeholders
- Loss of interest by senior management
- Lack of senior management support
- Progress reports not integrated with the plan
- Lack of Leader authority
- Poor action planning skills
- No planned progress meetings
- Progress reviews not signed off
- Poor problem solving skills
- No active evaluation of performance
- Clear deadline for project completion

It is essential that you ensure everyone involved with your project has clear instructions on the reporting procedures you want and the methods of measurement you are using for assessing progress and the extent of completion of each work package. Failure on these aspects of the project, through assuming people will know how to perform, can lead to a state of confusion that results in weakened co-operation. Teamwork suffers in this climate, project members avoid helping each other and become insulated and you lose effective control of the project.

The Stakeholders

Many projects are perceived to run into serious problems due to the failure to identify and value the stakeholders. You run the serious risk of interference at any time during the project life cycle if you have ignored this essential step. The list can change as the project progresses. The Leader's checklist identifies many of the key actions you must take with the stakeholders and ignoring these will certainly add to your problems eventually. Most projects do not have a clear end date, where the team can suddenly fragment and return (hopefully) to their previous roles and jobs. Some difficulties include:

- Changes of expectations
- Unclear priorities
- Changing levels of involvement
- Unwillingness to co-operate
- Unwillingness to fulfil assigned responsibilities
- Lack of compliance with agreed procedures
- Exerting undue influence on senior management
- Loss of enthusiasm
- Procrastination in decision taking
- Lack of interest in team and personal objectives
- Avoiding resolution of inter-functional conflicts
- Excessive involvement with project detail
- Lack of knowledge and experience

You are most likely to be involved in the implementation of the outcomes of your project, taking on a co-ordination role. Such implementation will have a separate phased plan when a new set of stakeholders could surface. These may be the people who are responsible for carrying out the everyday operational activities using the products or outcomes of your project. They may be in sales, administration or production, but they will only now become involved. Their representative will usually have been an original stakeholder and now you will need to ensure these other people becoming involved are kept well informed by your project team. These new stakeholders are facing the problems of getting the project outcomes to work and will make heavy demands on your time. Keeping the project progressing at the same time as meeting these new demands is difficult and will require all your leadership skills for a successful implementation.

The project leader and team performance

Leading a project is hard work. If you do not believe this now and accept that success is initially in your hands, then you should look for a different role. Your enthusiasm, personal drive and ability to lead a team are fundamental attributes which create the appropriate climate for effective teamworking. Lack of understanding of all skills needed to manage a project through the four phases of the life cycle generates a low confidence level in the team. You cannot and should not expect the team to compensate for your own deficiencies, because this will inevitably lead to conflict. Other difficulties include:

- Lack of experience
- Lack of technical knowledge
- Lack of clear roles [you and the team]
- Lack of self-confidence
- Unclear objectives
- Little enthusiasm or commitment
- Team members already overloaded
- Poor inter-personal skills
- Inability to cope with changes
- Limited team experience
- Uneven distribution of work
- Little or no monitoring
- Procrastination over decisions

You will always be faced with occasions where you need to adopt an authoritative style in the interests of the project. Whenever possible you must involve your team in making decisions to create ownership. This is a significant contributing factor to teamwork and their performance through the commitment created. You still take the final decision as you have the authority. You set the standards of performance for the project both for yourself and the team and maintaining these to keep the project moving on the right track is the key to your ultimate success.

Summary

- *Be aware of the actions you take that have a direct contribution to project success*
- *Identify the essential factors for success*
- *Maintain a high level of concern for the factors that affect success at each phase of the LIFE CYCLE*
- *Take positive steps to avoid the common difficulties experienced with project teams*
- *Adopt a style appropriate to the situation to maintain performance*

12

Critical Success Factors

Achieving success is part of your driving force towards realising your personal objectives. All the members of your team have their own personal objectives and their drive and energy will be directed towards achieving success if they can see these objectives are likely to be satisfied. At an early stage of the planning phase of any project it is valid to spend some time with your team assessing the factors which will be measured as an indication of success. Some of these factors are critical to any project achieving success, others you must derive specifically for your project. So the Critical Success Factors are derived on two levels:

- **LEVEL 1 – PROCESS FACTORS**
  – apply to any project
- **LEVEL 2 – PROJECT FACTORS**
  – apply to your project

There are obviously many factors which can be said to contribute to you achieving success but there is an essential minimum list of criteria which are critical. Your initial concern must be to arrive at a clear statement of the project objectives.

Setting the project objectives

Objectives are often confused with aims and organisational mission statements. The latter is really a statement that pulls together the relationship between the resources, activities and customers of an organisation. The project objectives describe the position the organisation desires to achieve with respect to specific resources, activities and customers.

These objectives must be:

- Specific, i.e. not broad or of a general nature
- Measurable, i.e. tangible and able to be verified practically
- Achievable, i.e. attainable in the prevailing environment
- Realistic, i.e. possible with known available resources
- Timed, i.e. given carefully designated timescales

You must verify that the objectives are also consistent with corporate strategy. Unfortunately, not all these characteristics are always immediately obvious in project objectives statements. Soft projects particularly have problems in establishing firm objectives until after all the possible alternatives have been explored and management decisions taken. In these circumstances you must continually review the objectives, amending them as the work progresses.

The Objectives Statement

The objectives statement must have the characteristics listed and presented in a manner that allows them to be easily understood by everybody involved with the project. It represents the framework for the scope of work to be carried out to achieve desired results for the organisation. You need to derive a statement containing vital information that everybody accepts as valid and that receives stakeholder approval and ownership. There are five elements you should consider as a minimum:

- **The perceived problem or need**

    The problem or need which has been identified as the source of the project is frequently based on perceived effects. It is always valid to examine this for underlying causes at an early stage to ensure you clearly understand the problem you are attempting to resolve. Failure to do this could lead you to make erroneous decisions in the planning phase.

■ **The purpose of deriving a solution**

You should make a simple statement of the organisational need to create a project for resolving the need or problem. If there is no clear purpose then whey are you doing it at all?

■ **The benefits expected from deriving a solution**

There are always benefits to be derived from any change, although not everyone is necessarily happy or in agreement with that change. However the project is being established to satisfy strategic organisational needs, so the benefits can be identified. These must be accepted and agreed with stakeholders, who will usually have a significant input to their perceptions of potential benefits. Always ensure that benefits you list can be measured.

■ **Definition of the results to be achieved**

Having established purpose and benefits it should not be too difficult for you to define the more specific detail of the actual results to be achieved. These may be phased through the project, yielding cumulative benefits that you can identify. The results are the minimum acceptable for the project to be recognised as successful by the key stakeholders.

■ **The deadlines for achieving the results**

In the final part of the objectives statement you set out the timescales for the project, identifying the milestone dates for completion of each phase and the various stages in each phase. You must be realistic in setting these deadlines, making adequate provision for unforeseen events with reasonable contingencies. The milestone dates will be key progress reporting points in the project and are often associated with key decisions and release of resources.

The objectives statement is the corner foundation stone supporting the fabric of your project. It is clearly relevant to give it adequate time and attention to ensure you get acceptance and commitment of the stakeholders to all the elements of the statement. Without this ownership your project is starting with a serious defect and the downstream consequences could be irreversible, with significant wastage of resources.

It is during the process of objectives setting that covert or hidden agendas sometimes surface and you cannot afford to ignore them. Awareness allows you to be prepared for later situations when such hidden motives could be used to influence decisions in the planning, organisation or execution of the project. They can be used to your advantage at times but equally they can be a source of blockage, creating barriers to progress and even on rare occasions outright sabotage! They may be personal to individuals or functional. In any organisation there is a tendency for departments to create a sub-culture of the organisational culture, influenced and directed by the manager. This is often the source of conflict across functional interfaces and you need to understand the differences that exist across the various interfaces you will need to influence at each phase of the project.

The project objectives statement is therefore your primary

critical success factor and the key to setting the success criteria specific to your project.

Process Factors

The process factors are primarily concerned with strategic and tactical issues associated with getting the project to the point of implementation and then keeping things on track. Your failure to give these particular attention will put success at risk and lead to much time being spent on problem solving and resolving conflict arising from poor performance. These are listed in Fig. 12.1.

1.   The project objectives

Implementing a new project is an expensive use of organisational time, energy and money. A clearly defined sense of direction is essential with easily understood objectives which can be seen to be an integral part of the organisation's corporate objectives.

2.   Senior management support

The initial enthusiasm for the project at the senior level must be maintained at all times. Many projects are seen to drift aimlessly because of senior managers losing interest due to new priorities, devaluation of the project outcomes, dissociation from a perceived potential failure or even a sudden awareness that the project is pointless. Ongoing support from above is an essential ingredient to success.

3.   Stakeholder Consultations

The stakeholders include many people whom you must give time to consult and take their guidance and advice. Whether outside or inside your organisation, each believes

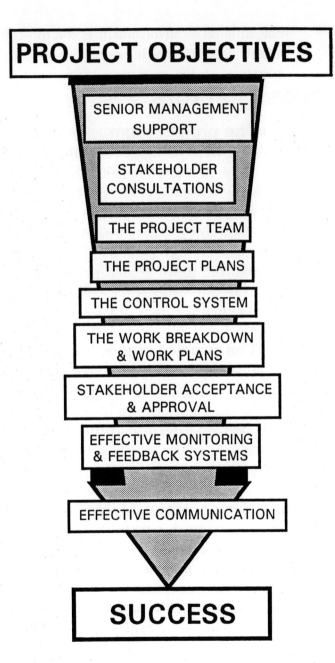

Fig. 12.1   Critical Success Factors

their little bit of involvement is the most important part. Identifying their needs, expectations and constraints is obligatory at the start and throughout the project life cycle.

4. The project team

It is not always possible to identify all the skills you need for your project as you start. As planning proceeds these needs are focused more clearly. It may be possible to form a small core team shortly after you are appointed to lead the project. Ensure you have a say in the selection of the core team members – you will be spending a lot of your time working with them. Establish clearly your own authority in dealing with people problems as well as your authority on the technical aspects of the project.

5. The project plans

No project can have a high probability of success unless planning is effective and detailed. The plans must be realistic with all the work defined and effective tracking methods agreed and defined. Problem solving and trouble-shooting procedures must be established to respond rapidly to any crises that occur.

6. The control system

You are appointed to lead a project and control it to move in a designed direction and achieve specific outcomes or results. To do this effectively you must establish a system for monitoring and tracking the progress, measuring the outcomes at regular intervals and comparing with the base plan. Variance measurement is a key activity to keep the project under your control. To do this you must agree working practices and procedures to be adopted by the team for your project. Be prepared to devalue traditional methods and customise these procedures to suit your project.

7.   The work breakdown and tasks

The work and all tasks must be identified along with their inter- dependencies. Each team member must understand their responsibility and you must be sure they have the skills and confidence to carry out their tasks to the standards of performance and quality you demand. The success of your project is very dependent on effective organisation of the work and the administration of the project throughout the execution phase. Frequently you will be forced to replan parts of the project or even complete the planning of the later stages of the project while the first stages have been started. This may require you to delegate part of your project authority to someone else so that you can maintain the overview.

8.   Stakeholder acceptance and approval

Throughout the project you will be seeking agreement and approvals from some or all stakeholders on a wide range of issues and activities. The true test of your success is your ability to maintain good relations with all stakeholders at all times AND satisfy their expectations and project objectives. This means good communication links are necessary with key people. Remember a satisfied client is potentially repeat business!

9.   Effective monitoring and feedback systems

Every step along the planned path of the project must be monitored and procedures clearly defined for performance feedback. This links in to the tracking process and the project control system. But plans are just a statement of intent, you must make it all happen and keep checking that it does. This requires you to have regular contact with each team member as well as the stakeholders, ensuring there are no problems or conflicts arising which need your attention.

10. Communication

The project machine has key components and many moving parts that contribute to smooth running. But few machines can run for long without a source of power input or regular lubrication. This is provided by communication, keeping all the parts informed of what is happening on the project with regular reviews, resolving problems and hold-ups promptly. Without this climate of open communication the project will start to 'overheat' allowing conflicts to arise and effort wasted through being directed at resolving differences. There is no movement in a vacuum except random movement!

Project Factors

The 'Project Factors' are derived from the Objectives Statement derived at the conception phase of the project. You have agreed the results to be achieved and the expectations of all identified stakeholders are known. You have to decide how you and the team will measure your progress towards meeting these demands in practice. Through monitoring and control you will receive status reports and progress information at regular intervals that is entered into your tracking procedures to show progress against the base plan.

It is essential to decide the measurement criteria to be used and ensure that everyone understands how these are to be used and applied. It is pointless to state a success factor which no one can actually measure or which allows excessive conflict to arise in the team. Any measurement is subjective and reflects on individual performance and it is important that you take time to ensure that team acceptance and ownership is generated.

At the same time you must ensure that the stakeholders give their approval to the factors to be measured and the criteria to be used. Since you are accountable for the work done such approval should not be unreasonably withheld. This requires you to influence and even, on occasions negotiate agreement with stakeholders. Your degree of success depends on your understanding of them, their changing needs and expectations and their prevailing situation at the time. At the outset it is valuable if you ask yourself two important questions:

- What is not negotiable under any circumstances?

- Where am I prepared to agree a compromise in the project's interest?

The spectrum of agreement ranges from total agreement, through various levels of agreement with reservations, i.e. consensus, to total disagreement and maybe outright, vigorous opposition. In most circumstances an agreement is not difficult to achieve provided you have done your homework and made the effort to understand the stakeholder's viewpoint and the underlying reasons for it. Just like you, they are busy people too and have their priorities, so your judgement of timing could be crucial to achieving your purpose.

Summary

- *Identify the Critical Success Factors*
    - *the PROCESS factors*
    - *the PROJECT factors*
- *Ensure these are clear and understandable*
- *Seek stakeholder acceptance and approval*
- *Derive project success factors from the objectives statement*
- *Ensure everyone is clear how project success factors are to be measured and accept they are realistic and achieveable*

13

Effective Teamworking

Your potential for success in achieving the project objectives is dependent on the effective working of your team. Since the team is often made up of a group of people brought together specifically for your project, there is a high probability that they have not worked together before. In practice they may not even know each other except as a face in another department or section. This puts an additional burden on you initially to start the process of teambuilding to steer the group towards your objective of effective teamwork.

Some of the actions you can take have been reviewed in the development of the Project Leader's checklist (see Section 10) and clearly the group of people you have selected or had imposed on the project must have a common understanding of the project objectives. This sharing and acceptance of objectives is the primary step from 'a group' to 'a team'. Their *'raison d'être'* is then clarified as making things happen to achieve the desired results. This creates a need which is satisfied in the short term by team motivation and in the long term by success. Your role is to create the right 'climate' which does not just allow this to happen, but is carefully designed to ensure it can and will happen.

What is teamwork?

All organisations depend on people working together in harmony to achieve results. If people are to work together in this way it suggests that the team can accomplish more than the total output of the individual people, yet in practice this is often not the perception or reality. The team may exist but the teamwork is absent so that sometimes individuals actually work against each other. Teamwork is about a group of individuals working together to accomplish more than they would as individuals. The success of the team depends on the skills each individual has and the way you utilise the skills to produce a united effort. To achieve this you need the individuals in the team to support and work with each other, guided and supported by you to maintain a sense of focus and clear direction. Just like any sports team a prerequisite to good teamwork is the right mix of skills and a perceived lack of essential skills will lead to frustration and demotivation.

One of your critical success factors has been identified as the team and its effectiveness. You have to use your skills as a leader to rapidly form a group of people into a team or working unit.

The Effective Team

To make your team effective you must have a high regard for relationships and understand the team members as individuals. This is part of your efforts to create the right climate of openness which contributes to the building of mutual trust and respect between you and the team. The project team is characterised by its transitory nature, existing as a team for anything from a few weeks to many months. The individuals then return to other or previous jobs and the team concept has apparently broken down. In reality each individual in the team has learned something about teamwork and the steps towards becoming an effective team. This is beneficial to the organisation and helps make project teambuilding easier the next time. The process is self-generating to eventually achieve a large number of people who have project and teamwork experience.

The success of a project team is generally accepted as being measured by:

- Meeting the agreed objectives
- Performance to agreed deadlines
- Performance to agreed budgets for all resources

To achieve this you can identify some characteristics which you can take specific actions to create in your team:

- Clear understanding and acceptance of project objectives
- Clear definition of responsibilities and authority
- Commitment to the project
- Desire to achieve results
- Participation and involvement in planning and decisions
- Opportunity for creativeness
- Conditions for effective problem solving

- Flexible attitude and willingness to accept change
- Interesting and challenging work
- High concern for standards and quality
- Constructive approach to resolving conflict
- Good communication and feedback processes
- Opportunities for personal development to learn new skills
- Open and regular performance review – team and individual
- Clear procedures for inter-functional communication and working
- Accepted project planning and organisational procedures
- Positive use of criticism and confrontation as developmental
- Good team spirit – encouraging self help and working relationships

This may seem a formidable list of action points for you, yet most of these you do anyway, often without a conscious decision. But you have a fledgling team and you must address each of the above actions and any others relevant to your organisation or the project. This is not just a 'one-off' activity as you will continue to seek to improve teamworking through regular monitoring, maintenance and review. This is the third dimension of your role - Managing Performance, which creates that climate for your team that is special and is perceived by others as striving for excellence.

Barriers to performance

If there are many things you can do to ensure team effectiveness there are some key areas which are likely to cause significant interference with your attempts to build a successful team. These are:

- Unclear objectives for the project
- Lack of strategic direction
- Inadequate resources, both quantity and quality
- Senior management apathy, loss of interest or opposition
- Power games and unclear channels of authority
- Conflicts left unresolved
- Lack of job security
- Uncertain and changing priorities
- Moving the goal posts

You clearly cannot control all these factors effectively but you can influence them to varying amounts in the interests of your project. Certainly any signals you receive at any time that any problems are developing in these areas must prompt you to take some positive action. The downstream effect on the project and your team could be disastrous if you fail to react to any such signs. The final potential barrier to good teamwork and project success is, of course, your leadership and particularly your own style which influences team motivation and the drive to achieve success.

Teambuilding

Teambuilding is essential at the start of the project, but it is also an ongoing process throughout the project. You must continuously monitor the team performance and openly discuss process problems with team members to seek every opportunity to improve. Discuss team functioning with the Accountable Executive to identify perceptions of performance from the stakeholders' viewpoint. Take corrective action promptly. Regular team meetings are essential as well as regular 1:1 sessions with each team member to ensure there are no problems or conflicts developing.

Your ultimate objective is to build a high performance team. You will have noticed the similarity between the factors that interfere with team performance and the key process factors which were discussed in Section 12 as the Critical Success Factors.

High performance and success do not just happen, you must make them happen and this summarises all the aspects of the role discussed here.

Summary

- *Create a climate for effective teamwork*
- *Integrating the team members into a working unit must be a high priority for you*
- *Maintain a concern for the essential characteristics of an effective team – take appropriate actions to achieve them*
- *Be concernd about the potential barriers to good performance and take steps to minimise their affects on your team*
- *Successful teamwork does not appear – you mut make it happen*

Appendix 1
Glossary of Project
Management Terms

There is a considerable amount of jargon used by project managers today, enhanced by the rapid growth in the use of personal computers for planning and control of projects. The list gives some of the more common terms and their usual meaning.

A

ACCOUNTABLE EXECUTIVE. The individual, usually a senior manager, who is held to account for the success of a project.

ACTION CYCLE. The dynamic reiterative process of actions that a leader follows to achieve results.

ACTIVITY. A clearly defined task with known duration: often used to include a series of tasks which together complete a particular step or part of the work.

ACTIVITY ON ARROW DIAGRAM. A network diagram where all activities are represented by arrows and events represented by circles.

ACTIVITY ON NODE DIAGRAM. A network diagram where all activities are represented by the node or event, usually as a box, and the arrows are used merely to show the logical flow of the project.

ARROW. The symbol by which an activity in the Arrow Diagram.

ARROW DIAGRAM. A diagrammatic statement of the complete project by means of arrows: also known as a **Network Diagram**.

B

BACKWARD PASS. The procedure by which the latest event times or the finish and start times for the activities of a network are determined.

C

CIRCLE. The symbol used to represent an event, i.e. the start or finish of an activity.

CONTROL SYSTEM. The procedures established at the start of the project that provide the Leader with the necessary data to compare planned status with the actual status at any instant in time, to identify variances and take corrective action.

CPM. Critical Path Method – a system where activities are represented by arrows on a diagram which can then be used for effective planning of the use of resources and subsequent control of the project.

CRITICAL PATH. The sequence of activities which determines the total time for the project. All activities on the critical path are known as **Critical Activities**.

CRITICAL SUCCESS FACTORS. The factors that have a direct impact on the success of a project.

D

DEPENDENCY. The basic rule of logic governing network drawing – any activity which is dependent on another must be shown to emerge from the HEAD event of the activity on which it depends.

DUMMY. A logical link, but which represents no specific operation [zero resources].

DURATION. The estimated or actual time to complete an activity.

E

EET. The earliest event time – the earliest completion time for an event which does not effect the **Total Project Time**.

EFT. The earliest finish time of an activity without changing total time or the spare or float time.

EVENT. A point in the progress of the project after total completion of all preceding activities.

F

FLOAT. Difference between the time necessary and the time available for an activity.

FORWARD PASS. The procedure for determining the earliest event times of a network.

G

GANTT CHART. A graphical method of showing a project

schedule which shows project time, dates, all activities, resources and their relationships.

H

HARD PROJECT. A project with clearly defined objectives and readily identifiable resource requirements from the outset.

HEAD EVENT. The event at the finish of an activity. The event then changes its nature and becomes the **Tail Event** for the succeeding activity.

K

KEY STAGE. A group of closely related activities that can be isolated together as a clear stage of the project which must be complete before passing to the next stage.

L

LET. The latest time by which an event can be achieved without affecting the Total Project Time from start to finish.

LFT. The latest possible finish time without changing the total task or float times.

M

MILESTONE. Another name for an event, but usually reserved for a significant or major event in the project. Often used for identifying key progress reporting points.

MULTI-LEVEL PLANNING. Planning the project at several levels of detail, starting with the key stages and then exploding each key stage to show all the associated activities. Where necessary any activity is further exploded to show further detail of associated tasks at the next level down and so on.

MUST DATE. A planned date when an activity or group of activities must be complete under all circumstances.

N

NODE. Another name for an event.

P

PRECEDENCE DIAGRAM. A network where activity and dependency is shown by a box to represent the activity and an arrow to show the dependency link or logic. The arrows only serve to show the flow of the project between the nodes.

PREDECESSOR. The activity immediately prior to an event.

PROJECT LIFE CYCLE. A systems approach to a project where the project is described as passing through four phases from conception to termination.

R

RESOURCE. Anything other than time which is needed for carrying out an activity.

RESOURCE LEVELLING. Utilisation of available float within a network to ensure that resources required are appreciably constant.

RESOURCE SMOOTHING. The scheduling of activities within the limits of their total floats to minimise fluctuations in resource requirements.

S

SEMI-CRITICAL PATH. That path which is next to the critical path when all paths are arranged in order of float.

SLACK. Used to refer only to an event and is the latest date [time] minus the earliest date [time].

SOFT PROJECT. A project where the objectives are only broadly stated and the resources needed are unknown and flexible, the scope left open intentionally and deadlines not defined clearly.

SPONSOR. The senior manager who takes ownership of the project on behalf of the organisation.

STAKEHOLDER. Any individual who has an interest or stake in the project at any time during the project life cycle.

SUB-CRITICAL PATH. A path which is not critical.

SUCCESSOR. The activity immediately following an event.

T

TAIL EVENT. The event at the beginning of an activity.

TAIL SLACK. The slack possessed by an event at the tail of an activity.

TIME LIMITED SCHEDULING. The scheduling of activities such that the specified project time is not exceeded using resources to a predetermined pattern.

TOTAL FLOAT. The total float possessed by an activity.

TRACKING. The process of taking progress information gathered in a control system and inserting this into the original plan to show the actual status, i.e. the compliance or deviation from the planned status of the project at that point in time.

W

WORK BREAKDOWN STRUCTURE. The diagrammatic presentation of all the key stages and their associated activities arranged in a hierarchical format, showing each level of planning.

Appendix 2
Bibliography

Critical Path Analysis & Other Project Network Techniques
4th Edition 1984, KEITH LOCKYER, PITMAN, London

BRITISH STANDARDS INSTITUTION
BS 4335: 1972 Glossary of Terms used in project Network Techniques
BS 6046: Parts 1, 2, 3, 4. Use of network techniques in project management

NETWORK ANALYSIS FOR PLANNING AND SCHEDULING
3rd Edition, 1978. A. BATTERSBY, MACMILLAN, London

ADVANCED PROJECT MANAGEMENT
F.L. HARRISON, GOWER PRESS, Aldershot 1981

CPM IN CONSTRUCTION MANAGEMENT
J.J. O'BRIEN, McGRAW-HILL, New York 1971

PROJECT COST CONTROL USING NETWORKS
2nd Edition, 1980, C. STAFFURTH, HEINEMANN, London

PLANNING BY NETWORK
3rd Edition, 1977. H.S. WOODGATE, BUSINESS BOOKS, London

SUCCESSFUL PROJECT MANAGEMENT
M.D. ROSENAU, Jr., VAN NOSTRAND REINHOLD, New York

THE MANAGER AS A LEADER
THE INDUSTRIAL SOCIETY, London

PLANNING PROJECTS
20 Steps To Effective Planning of Projects
THE INDUSTRIAL SOCIETY

Appendix 3
Training

The Industrial Society offers training in the skills of project management through two public courses:

- Leading Projects
- Planning, Organising & Controlling Projects

Both courses give you the opportunity to learn the essential skills through discussion and practical work with people from a broad spectrum of businesses. The content is focused on giving both technical and non-technical people the skills of leading and managing a project in an understandable way which can be applied to any type or size of project. No formal previous training is necessary although both courses can effectively be used for revision and update of skills not practised for some time. Both programmes are structured to encourage maximum participation with step by step exercises and group work.

In addition, in-house training workshops can be conducted on your premises to focus directly on your specific needs. Such workshops have the added benefit of allowing participants to practise the skills learned on real-time projects as case studies during the training. Company systems for project organisation, planning and control can be derived in the workshop through facilitated consultation with all those involved in project work. The range of topics which can be included in such customised workshops extends beyond the programmes of public courses.

The Industrial Society also offers consultancy services from Management Advisers with extensive relevant experience. The activities range from advising and designing organisational structures and systems for project work to supporting a project team on real-time projects from conception through to completion. Such services are also available for many other aspects of management development, skills enhancement and consultancy.

For further information please contact:

The Industrial Society
Peter Runge House
3, Carlton House Terrace
LONDON SW1Y 5DG
Telephone: 071 839 4300